Communications
in Computer and Information Scie

Alessandro Moschitti
Barbara Plank (Eds.)

Trustworthy Eternal Systems via Evolving Software, Data and Knowledge

Second International Workshop, EternalS 2012
Montpellier, France, August 28, 2012
Revised Selected Papers

 Springer

Volume Editors

Alessandro Moschitti
Barbara Plank
University of Trento
Department of Information Engineering and Computer Science
Via Sommarive, 5, 38123 Povo, Trento, Italy
E-mail: {moschitti, barbara.plank}@disi.unitn.it

ISSN 1865-0929   e-ISSN 1865-0937
ISBN 978-3-642-45259-8   e-ISBN 978-3-642-45260-4
DOI 10.1007/978-3-642-45260-4
Springer Heidelberg New York Dordrecht London

Library of Congress Control Number: 2013954722

CR Subject Classification (1998): I.2, D.2, H.3, H.4

Typesetting: Camera-ready by author, data conversion by Scientific Publishing Services, Chennai, India

Printed on acid-free paper

Springer is part of Springer Science+Business Media (www.springer.com)

Preface

Latest research within ICT has made it possible to pinpoint the most important and urgently required features that future systems should possess to meet users' needs. Accordingly, methods making systems capable of adapting to changes in user requirements and application domains have been pointed out as key research areas. Adaptation and evolution depend on several dimensions, e.g., time, location, and security conditions, expressing the diversity of the context in which systems operate. A design based on an effective management of these dimensions constitutes a remarkable step towards the realization of *Trustworthy Eternal Systems*.

The second international workshop on Trustworthy Eternal Systems via Evolving Software, Data and Knowledge (EternalS) was held on August 28, 2012 in conjunction with ECAI 2012, the biennial and leading European Conference on Artificial Intelligence. The workshop aimed at bringing together worldwide stakeholders and their related communities to discuss current research trends on the use of intelligent techniques for effective and efficient design of software systems. Additionally, the program of the workshop hosted an invited talk by Hendrick Blockeel from the University of Leuven, Belgium, who gave an overview of current and future trends in machine learning and data mining.

The workshop issued a call for high-quality contributions in the areas mentioned above that resulted in numerous high-quality submissions. Out of them, ten interdisciplinary papers were selected for inclusion in these post-proceedings through a rigorous peer review process. The papers are organized into three main sections:

1. Natural Language Processing (NLP) for Software Systems, which proposed the use of NLP techniques for automatic software construction. The techniques proposed in the four papers range from automatic analysis of software requirements to software testing.
2. Machine Learning for Software Systems, which focused on the use of machine learning for very diverse software applications, ranging from porting and making secure software, e.g., in the cloud, to improving the performance of software for networked devices.
3. Roadmap for future research, which discussed concrete proposals of interesting future research by also presenting the second-year road-map of EternalS.

We thank the authors for their contribution in this volume and the members of the Program Committee for timely and insightful reviews.

January 2013

Alessandro Moschitti
Barbara Plank
Program Chairs

Organization

Program Chairs

Alessandro Moschitti   University of Trento, Italy
Barbara Plank   University of Trento, Italy

Program Committee

Andreas Andreou	University of Cyprus, Cyprus
Lefteris Angelis	Aristotle University of Thessaloniki, Greece
Roberto Basili	University of Rome Tor Vergata, Italy
Helen Berki	University of Tampere, Finland
Anna Corazza	University of Naples Federico II, Italy
Sergio Di Martino	University of Naples Federico II, Italy
Michael Felderer	University of Innsbruck, Austria
Fausto Giunchiglia	University of Trento, Italy
Falk Howar	TU Dordtmund, Germany
Valerie Issarny	Inria, France
Richard Johansson	University of Gothenburg, Sweden
George Kakarontzas	Technical University of Larisa, Greece
Achilles Kameas	Hellenic Open University, Greece
Basel Katt	University of Innsbruck, Austria
Emilia Mendes	University of Auckland, New Zealand
Riccardo Scandariato	Katholieke Universiteit Leuven, Belgium
Ina Schaefer	TU Braunschweig, Germany
Holger Schner	Software Competence Center Hagenberg, Austria
Christos Tjortjis	The University of Manchester, United Kingdom
Grigorios Tsoumakas	Aristotle University of Thessaloniki, Greece
Maria Virvou	University of Piraeus, Greece

Table of Contents

Semantic and Algorithmic Recognition Support to Porting Software Applications to Cloud

Beniamino Di Martino and Giuseppina Cretella

Second University of Naples - Dept. of Industrial and Information Engineering, Italy
beniamino.dimartino@unina.it, giuseppina.cretella@gmail.com

Abstract. This paper presents a methodology, a technique and an ongoing implementation, aimed at supporting software porting (i.e. to adapt the software to be used in different execution environments), from object oriented domain towards Cloud Computing. The technique is based on semantic representation of Cloud Application Programming Interfaces, and on automated algorithmic concept recognition in source code, integrated by structural based matchmaking techniques. In particular the following techniques are composed and integrated: automatic recognition of the algorithms and algorithmic concepts implemented in the source code and the calls to libraries and APIs performing actions and functionalities relevant to the target environment; comparison through matchmaking of the recognized concepts and APIs with those present in the functional ontology which describes the target API; mapping of the source code excerpts and the source calls to APIs to the target API calls and elements.

Keywords: Semantic Discovery, Cloud APIs, Cloud Resources, Algorithmic Recognition.

1 Introduction

Software porting over different domains is an important issue, mainly in the recent years, where porting operation are needed not only for the reingeenerization of old applications, but mostly to port applications over different technologies, like Cloud Computing.

In the last years Cloud Computing has emerged as a prominent model to provide online access to computational resources, thanks to its characteristics of scalability, elasticity, reduced cost, easiness of use, simple maintenance. The concept of cloud computing is clearly expressed by the NIST definition: "Cloud computing is a model for enabling ubiquitous, convenient, on-demand network access to a shared pool of configurable computing resources (e.g., networks, servers, storage, applications, and services) that can be rapidly provisioned and released with minimal management effort or service provider interaction.[...]"

One of the issues related to the adoption of the cloud computing paradigm is the lackness of a common programming model and open standard interfaces. Many cloud providers offer different cloud services, but each of their offerings is

A. Moschitti and B. Plank (Eds.): EternalS 2013, CCIS 379, pp. 1–15, 2013.

based on proprietary Application Programming Interfaces (APIs). This situation complicates the already challenging task of building up applications from interoperable services provided by different cloud providers; and the specific APIs, kind of resources and services provided by a given cloud provider make future migrations costly and difficult (Cloud Vendor Lock in). Portability of code towards a Cloud providers' environment and among Cloud providers' environments is a severe issue today.

The application of semantic techniques to reverse engineering can enable the automation or automated support of activities such as porting. Understanding the functionalities exposed by software artifacts represents an essential support for a large range of software reengineering activities such as maintenance, debugging, reuse, modernization, and porting.

This paper presents a methodology, a technique and the ongoing implementation, aimed at supporting software porting towards Cloud Computing environments. The technique is based on semantic representation of Cloud Application Programming Interfaces, and on automated Algorithmic Concept Recognition in source code, integrated by structural based matchmaking techniques.

We combine techniques such as graph based source code representation, first-order-logic rules for algorithmic recognition and semantic based algorithmic and codes (APIs) knowledge representation.

Objectives of the described work relate porting of applications towards Cloud through the extraction of knowledge from the Application Programming Interfaces, and the association of semantic description identifying the concepts they implement. The described technique anyway can target a wide range of applications, from code reuse to advanced code searching.

The paper is organized as follows. In Section 2 we will present an overview of works related to reverse engineering solution for program comprehension, with particular attention to the works that use ontologies and graph based representations for code and software artifacts. In Section 3 we will present the porting methodology, based on an automatic analysis and representation of code at higher level of abstraction than the syntactical and structural one. Section 4 presents the main components of the architecture and the workflow of the methodology presented in the previous section. Conclusions and future works are drawn in Section 5.

2   Background and Related Work

Reverse engineering is the process of system analysis to identify the components and their interrelationships and create representations at a higher level of abstraction. Therefore it's an activity that allows getting specific information about the design of a system from its code, through extraction and abstraction of system information. Reverse engineering may require a thorough understanding of systems (white-box approach) or may be limited to only the external interfaces (software reengineering of black-box). The white-box approach supports reverse engineering with a deep understanding of individual modules and conversion activities. The black-box approach is limited to the study of the external interfaces of systems and activities of encapsulation (wrapping). In reverse engineering various software artifacts can be analysed. A software artifact is any tangible product created during software development. Some artifacts (e.g. use cases, class diagrams and other UML models, requirements and design documents) are useful to describe functions, architecture and software design. Others involve the development process itself, such as project plans, business cases and risk assignment. The code, the released executable and the associated documentation are artifact too. There are two different directions in program comprehension research: the first strives for understanding the cognitive processes that programmers use when they understand programs and use empirical information to produce a variety of theories that provide explanations of how programmers understand programs, and can provide advice on how program comprehension tools and methods may be improved; the second aims at developing semi-automated tool support to improve program comprehension. Some of the more prominent approaches include textual, lexical and syntactic analysis (focus on the source code and its representations), execution and testing (based on observing program behaviour, including actual execution and inspection walkthroughs), graphic methods (including earlier approaches such as graphing the control flow of the program, the data flow of the program, and producing the program dependence graphs), domain knowledge based analysis (focus on recovering the domain semantics of programs by combining domain knowledge representation and source code analysis). The problem of associating concepts to code is not a problem amenable to be solved in its general formulation because the human-oriented concepts are inherently ambiguous, and their recognition is based on a priori knowledge of a particular domain. The problem can instead be solved under specific constraints and limitations, such as limiting the range of recognition at the algorithmic level [10]. A different approach is to understand the code through the analysis of the documentation associated with it, with text mining techniques that capture the concepts described in the documentation and connect them with the appropriate portions of code that implement [2]. The approach in [2] represents various software artifacts, including source code and documents as formal ontologies. The ontological reasoning services allow programmers not only to reason about properties of the software systems, but also to actively acquire and construct new concepts based on their current understanding; and introducing an ontology-based comprehension model and a supporting comprehension methodologies that characterize program comprehension as an iterative process of concept recognition and relationship discovery. Application developers often reuse code already developed for several reasons. The most common situation is accessing libraries of reusable components or putting them in the application framework. Unfortunately, many libraries and frameworks are not very intuitive to use, and libraries often lack a comprehensive API documentation and code examples that illustrate a particular feature or functionality. It is therefore useful to provide advanced tools for code search and suggestion. This issue is addressed generally representing code in a form suitable to perform computation and reasoning, as shown in [3], where the code is represented through an ontology to perform query that can be used to provide suggestion for library usage. The ontology formalism is used to represent software assets by building a knowledge base that is automatically populated with instances representing source-code artifacts. This approach uses this knowledge base to identify and retrieve relevant code snippets. To add formal semantic annotations, it's necessary to have a formal knowledge description processable and to an appropriate level of abstraction. This is not always available, so it would be useful to have tools that can extract this knowledge automatically or semi automatically from the sources of information. One of the major structured sources of knowledge are the public interfaces of libraries of a specific domain. However, a single API contains only a view of the particular domain and it's not generally sufficient to obtain a complete model of the domain. In addition, the APIs contain a significant amount of noise due to implementation details that combine with the representation of knowledge in the domain interfaces. In order to overcome these problems it's possible to base the extraction of domain knowledge on multiple APIs that cover the same domain. This issue is addressed in [4], where it is proposed an approach to extract domain knowledge capturing the commonalities among multiple API; the extraction is based on the frequency matching of given elements. In [5] an approach to learning domain ontologies from multiple sources associated with the software project, i.e., software code, user guide, and discussion forums is proposed. This technique do not simply deal with these different types of sources, but it goes one step further and exploits the redundancy of information to obtain better results. In [6] and [7] it is proposed a method for domain ontology building by extracting ontological knowledge from UML models of existing systems, by comparing the UML model elements with the OWL ones and derive transformation rules between the corresponding model elements. The aim of the process is to reduce the cost and time for building domain ontologies with the reuse of existing UML models.

3   The Methodology

The porting methodology we are presenting is based on an automatic analysis and representation of code at higher level of abstraction than the syntactical and structural one: namely the algorithmic or functional level.

The methodology assumes that the porting procedure can be realized by restructuring the code to be ported to a target environment (e.g. Cloud) with suitable calls to functionalities of a given *target* Application Programming Interface, implementing all functionalities needed to deploy and run the code on the environment.

The target API is assumed to be (manually) semantically described at the algorithmic and functional level, and annotated, with concepts described by means of an OWL based *functional ontology*.

It is also assumed that the code to be ported includes implementations of algorithms and functionalities included in the functional ontology, and calls or libraries and APIs, which do not (necessarily) correspond to the target API.

The main idea underlying the methodology is the following: to automatically recognize the algorithms and algorithmic concepts implemented in the source code and the calls to libraries and APIs performing actions and functionalities relevant to the target environment, compare through matchmaking the recognized concepts and APIs with those present in the functional ontology which describes the target API and semantically annotates its elements and calls, and by means of this matching, eventually map the source code excerpts and the source calls to APIs to the target API calls and elements.

The methodology represents the following components in a uniform, graph based, representation, the *knowledge base*:

- the *Target API*;
- the *Grounding Ontology*;
- the *Functional Ontology*;
- the source code *Call Graph*;
- the source code *API Graph*;
- the *Candidate API Ontology Graph*;
- the source code *Program Dependence Graph*;
- the source code *Abstract Program Representation Graph*.

The *Target API* is the Application Programming Interface towards which the porting activity is addressed. Examples are the APIs exposed by the Cloud providers, offering Cloud resources and services at Infrastructure, Platform and Application levels. The methodology assumes that this API is (manually) semantically annotated with concepts of the Functional Ontology.

The *Grounding Ontology* is a syntactical representation on an API. It represents a base to build semantic annotations of the *grounding concepts* (the syntactical elements of the API) with the Functional Ontology concepts.

The *Functional Ontology* represents a collection of concepts from the domain of Programming Algorithms and Data Structures [8], general purpose functionalities offered by libraries related to a given domain, such as Cloud Computing, and Design Patterns [9].

The *Call Graph* represents the calling relationships between the source codes procedures.

The *Candidate API Ontology* is an ontology automatically derived from an API by applying a set of graph transformation patterns, as for instance illustrated in [1].

The *Program Dependence Graph* is a structural level representation of a program, which represents dependence relationships (control and data) among the program statements. In our methodology we use a PDG representation slightly augmented with syntactical control and data dependence information.

The *Abstract Program Representation* represents the recognized algorithmic concepts in the source code and their structure, the relationships among them, and groundings within the source code.

The above defined knowledge base components can be grouped in three different levels for both the source and the target porting environments, as sketched in (Fig. 1). In the first level, the *grounding level*, there are the basic information extracted by parsing the source code to port, which are the *Source API Graph* (in the scenario we have an API to map over another API), the *Call Graph* and the *Program Dependence Graph* (in the scenario we have a source code to port) in the source environment and the *Target API Graph* in the target environment. In the *Functional and Algorithmic Concept Level* we have on the source side the *Abstract Program Representation Graph* and the *Candidate API Ontology Graph* witch represent the high level information derived respectively from the Program Dependence Graph and the Source API Graph. On the source side at functional and algorithm level we have the graph representation of the Functional Ontology. In the *Application Level* we have concepts related to the application domain which can be linked with functional and algorithmic concepts.

	Source Environment	Target Environment
Grounding Level	Souce API graph, Call Graph, Program Dependence Graph	Target API graph
Functional and Algorithmic concept Level	Abstract Program Representation Graph, Candidate Ontology API Graph	Functional Ontology graph (Application Pattern, Algorithm, Data Structure concepts)
Application Level		Application Domain Ontology

Fig. 1. Knowledge base levels

The source code is represented using two graph structures: the *Program Dependence Graph* suitable for algorithm recognition, discussed in Section 4.1, and another based on the *Call Graph* with one node for each call in the source code.

Given these representations, the methodology tries to find an equivalence of source code components and target API components, through graphical matchmaking of their graph based semantic representations. These are the Abstract Program representation and the Candidate API Ontology of the source code, and the functional ontology with which the target API components are represented and annotated.

The same approach can be used to find equivalent implementations of the same functionalities among different API. If the two APIs (source and target) are both semantically described and annotated with the functional ontology the equivalence is quite straightforward to find because the two annotations will refer to the same functional ontology concept; while if one of the two APIs is not annotated, we can produce the Candidate API ontology Graph and match it with the functional ontology, used to annotate the other API.

4 Design of the Architecture and Ongoing Implementation of the Porting Support Procedure

The architecture implementing the methodology described in the previous section, is illustrated in Fig. 2 with the workflow and interactions among the components, while Fig. 3 illustrates the workflow for the API annotation process.

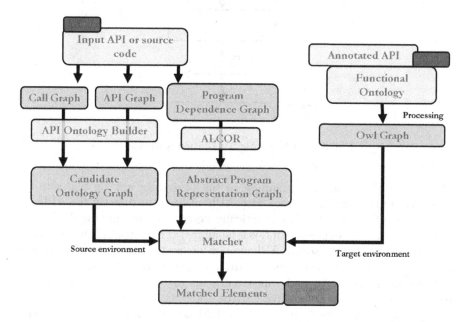

Fig. 2. Workflow of the porting procedure

The architecture is composed of the following four modules.

The *ALCOR (ALgorithmic COncept Recognizer)* module [10] recognizes algorithmic concepts in the code, producing the Abstract Program Representation.

The *API Ontology Builder* extracts the graph by parsing source code and from the graph representing the code produces the *API grounding ontology* which represent the base where to ground the semantic annotations. This ontology enables the annotation of the API elements in a simple way, by adding relation between grounding elements and high level abstraction concept. Additionally the API Ontology Builder produces the *Candidate API ontology* graph applying graph transformation patterns defined for the specific programming language or model.

The *Schema Matcher* module [14] accepts two graph based representations and performs the matching between the two graphs, by applying several algorithm including structural-based algorithms and syntactical ones.

The *Annotator* allows the user to semantically annotate the target API with concepts from the functional ontology.

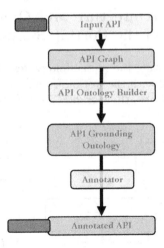

Fig. 3. API Semantic Annotation workflow

As illustrated in Fig. 2, the inputs to the procedure are, on one side the source code to be ported, together with APIs utilized, or directly the APIs; on the other side the target API, semantically described and annotated with the Functional Ontology (expressed in OWL language). The output of the procedure is a mapping between the source API components and source code excerpts, and target API components which are equivalent (functional equivalence) to the source elements and code, and which represent the candidates to replace the source elements during the porting activity.

The input components (source code and APIs) are statically analysed with use of a static code analyser, and the components of uniform the knowledge representation, the Program Dependence Graph, the Call Graph and the API Graph, are produced. On the other hand an OWL parser produces the OWL graph representation of the functional ontology. The ALCOR module detects, from the Program Dependence Graph, the algorithmic concepts implemented within the source code, and produces the Abstract Program Representation, represented as a graph in the uniform knowledge base, which represents the recognized concepts and their hierarchical and control/data dependences, and their grounding (implementation) within the source code. Details on the recognition procedure and the concepts representation are provided in sec. 4.1.

The API Ontology Builder module, on the other hand, analyzes the APIs used by the source code, represented by the API graph, and produces the *Candidate API ontology* graph, by applying graph transformation rule patterns defined for the specific programming language or model. This Ontology represents the semantics of the components of the API under analysis, and their semantic relationships. Details on the transformation rules and on the module implementation are provided in sec. 4.3.

Once produced the uniform Knowledge base with the components described, the Matcher performs the matching between the source and target elements, producing a set of mapping elements specifying the matching elements together with a similarity value between 0 (strong dissimilarity) and 1 (identity) indicating the plausibility of their correspondence.

The implementation of the porting support procedure is ongoing work, and it is mainly consisting of (a) the development of the API Ontology builder and API annotator; (b) the development of the source code analysis front end (starting from a previous implementation realized within the ROSE compiler construction toolkit; (c) the integration of the already developed modules ALCOR and Schema Matcher; (d) the implementation of a Graphical User Interface, providing the user with the matching results in a form graphically relating the source code excerpts with suggested target API elements, in order to perform a suitable and effective support to the porting activity.

In the following sections we describe in more details the working principles and the ongoing implementation and integration of the Algorithmic Concepts Recognition module (sec. 4.1), of the Schema Matcher module (sec. 4.2) and of the API Ontology Builder module (sec. 4.3).

4.1 Algorithmic Concepts Recognition

The *Algorithmic Concept Recognizer*, previously designed and developed [10,11] implements a technique for automated algorithmic concepts recognition in source code [12], where the definition of *parallelizable algorithmic concept* and the technique to describe and detect the algorithmic concepts by using an attributed grammar were presented, and which is briefly resumed here.

The Algorithmic Concepts Recognition is a Program Comprehension technique to recognize in source code the instances of known algorithms. The recognition strategy is based on a hierarchical parsing of algorithmic concepts. Starting from an intermediate representation of code, *Basic Concepts* are recognized first. Subsequently they become components of *Structured Concepts* in a hierarchical and / or recursive way. This abstraction process, can be modeled as a hierarchical parsing, by using *Concept Recognition Rules* that act on a description of concept instances found in the code.

Basic concepts. The building blocks of the hierarchical abstraction process are the *Basic Concepts*. They are chosen among the elements of the intermediate code representation at the structural level. A slightly modified version of the Program Dependence Graph is used: it is augmented with syntactical information (e.g. trees structures representing expressions for each statement node), control and data dependence information (e.g. control branches, data dependence level, variables, ... are added).

Concept Recognition Rules. The *Concept Recognition Rules* are the production rules of the parsing: they describe the set of characteristics and properties to permit the identification of an algorithmic concept instance in the code.

Each recognition rule related to an algorithmic concept specifies how subconcepts, formed by set of statements and variables linked by a functionality, are related and organized within a specific abstract control structure. Each rule describes the concept in a recursive way by using:

- A composition hierarchy: this is specified by the set of sub-concepts directly composing the concept and their own composition hierarchies.
- A set of constraints and conditions to be satisfied by the composing sub-concepts, and all the relationships among them and with the sub-concepts of the hierarchy.

A formalism for the specification of the recognition rules is given by *Attributed Grammars* [13] for their expressiveness regarding the specification of the hierarchy, the constraints and relationships, as is well-known for the specification of programming languages.

A production rule of the grammar specifies: a set *sub-concept* of terminal and non-terminal symbols which represent the set of sub-concepts forming the concept represented by the lhs symbol *concept*.

The set *condition* represent the relationships and constraints that must be fulfilled by the sub-concepts forming the concept, in order to be recognized as a valid instance.

The set *AttributionRule* of the production assigns values to the attributes of the recognized concept utilizing the values of attributes of the composing sub-concepts.

The syntax of a production rule is as follows:

Rule =
  rule *concept* →
    composition
      { *subconcept* }
    condition
      [**local** LocalAttributes]
      { Condition }
    attribution
      { AttributionRule }

LocalAttributes =
  attribute : Type { *attribute* : Type }

$concept \in N$
$subconcept \in N \cup T$
$attribute \in A$
$Condition \in C$
$AttributionRule \in R$

The Recognition Process. The PDG information, together with syntactical information can be produced as a set of Prolog facts representing the *Abstract Program Representation*. The hierarchical parsing process that do the recognition, is performed by an *Inferential Engine* that applies the production rules of the parsing (expressed as Prolog clauses) to the set of terminals, non-terminals and relationships of the *Abstract Program Representation*.

An overall *Abstract Program Representation* is generated during the recognition process. An example is illustrated in Fig. 4.

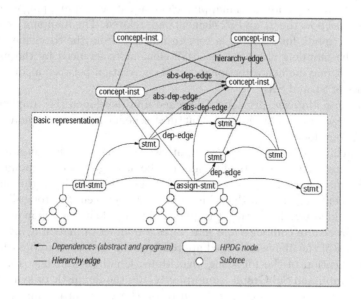

Fig. 4. Abstract Program Representation

It has the structure of a *Hierarchical PDG* (HPDG), reflecting the hierarchical strategy of the recognition process. As long as the parsing process proceeds and more and more abstract concepts are recognized, they are represented as nodes in increasingly higher layers of the HDPG. The nodes of this graph are connected by two kind of edges. The *hierarchy edges* connect each node representing a concept to the lower layer nodes representing its subconcepts. The graph structure determined by this kind of edges represents the hierarchy of abstraction; this structure is generally a tree, excepted in the case of shared concepts, i.e. when a concept instance is subconcept of more than one concept. The *dependence edges* link together nodes that have abstract control and data dependence relationships between them. Note that, during the recognition process, dependence edges for the newly created abstract concept nodes are inherited from those of the composing subconcept nodes in a way that is characteristic of each concept.

4.2   Schema Matcher

A fundamental operation in the manipulation of ontologies is *match*, which takes two ontologies as input and produces a mapping between elements of the two ontologies that correspond semantically. Match plays a central role in numerous applications, such as web-oriented data integration, electronic commerce, schema integration, schema evolution and migration, application evolution, data warehousing, database design, web site creation and management, and component-based development. A mapping is defined as a set of mapping elements, each of which indicates that certain elements of schema S1 are mapped to certain elements in S2. Furthermore, each mapping element can have a mapping expression which specifies how the S1 and S2 elements are related. The mapping expression may be directional, for example, a certain function from the S1 elements referenced by the mapping element to the S2 elements referenced by the mapping element, or it may be non-directional, that is, a relation between a combination of elements of S1 and S2.

The *Schema Matcher*, previously designed and developed [14], implements a technique based on syntactic and structural schema matching, among two or more input ontologies.

The matching procedure takes as input two schemas and determines a mapping indicating which elements of the input schemas logically correspond to each other. The match result is a set of mapping elements specifying the matching schema elements together with a similarity value between 0 (strong dissimilarity) and 1 (identity) indicating the plausibility of their correspondence. Our matching procedure combines and integrates a number of matching algorithms, adopting two of the above described approaches: the structural approach, based on the application of the following algorithms: Children Matcher [15], Leaves Matcher, Graph and SubGraph Isomorphism [16]; the linguistic or syntactic approach, based on application of: Edit Distance (Levenshtein Distance) [17] and Synonym Matcher (through WordNet [18] synonyms thesaurus).

4.3   API Ontology Builder

The production of the *Candidate API Ontology Graph* from the source code is performed by the *API Ontology Builder* module by applying graph transformation patterns defined for the specific programming language or model. We have defined a series of transformation rules for object oriented model aimed to extract and transform proper language elements in ontological relation. In [1] similar set of rules are described. Some of the defined rules are illustrated in the following:

- (APIClassNodeA) → (OwlNodeA)
  A node representing a class A in the API graph becomes an OWL class A in the candidate ontology graph.
- (APIClassMethodNodeA) → (OwlNodeA)
  A node representing a method A in the API graph becomes a class A in the candidate ontology graph.
- (APIParameterNodeA) → (OwlNodeA)
  A node representing a parameter A in the API graph becomes a class A in the candidate ontology graph.

- (APIClassNodeA ihneritsEdge APIClassNodeB) → (OwlNodeB subclassOf OwlNodeA)
  If a class A inherits a class B in the API graph, the relation becomes a subclassOf relation between the correspondent classes of the OWL graph.
- (APIClassNodeA hasAttributeEdge APIClassNodeB) → (OwlNodeA ObjectProperty: hasProperty OwlNodeB)
  If a class A has an attribute B in the API graph, the relation becomes an Object Property with label "hasProperyy" between the correspondent classes of the OWL graph.
- (APIClassNodeA hasMethodEdge APIClassMethodNodeB) → (OwlNodeA ObjectProperty: isDoer OwlNodeB)
  If a class A has a method B in the API graph, the relation becomes an Object Property with label "isDoer" between the correspondent elements of the OWL graph.
- (APIClassMethodNodeA hasMethod APIClassMethodNodeConstructorB and APIClassMethodNodeConstructorB hasInputParameter APIParameterNodeC) → (OwlNodeClassA ObjectProperty: hasProperty OwlClassC)
  If a class A has a constructor with some input parameters, in the owl graph there are Object Properties with label "hasProperty" between the correspondent elements.
- (APIClassMethodNodeA hasInputParameterEdge APIParameterNodeB) → (OwlNodeA ObjectProperty: actsOn OwlNodeB)
  If a method A has some input parameter, there are Object Properties with label "actsOn" between the correspondent elements on the OWL graph.
- (APIClassMethodNodeA hasReturnTypeEdge APIClassNodeB) → (OwlNodeA ObjectProperty: produce OwlNodeB)
  If a method A has a return type B there is an Object Property with label "produce" between the correspondent elements in the OWL graph.

5   Conclusion

In this paper we have proposed an approach to perform automatically, or with automated support, operations like the alignment and mapping of software which will be useful to perform software modernization and migration. The methodology is based on an automatic analysis and representation of code at higher level of abstraction than the syntactical and structural one that enables automatic recognition of the algorithms and algorithmic concepts implemented in the source code. Based on matchmaking techniques, the concepts recognized are compared with functional concepts represented by the ontologies and the results provide useful information to perform porting of source code excerpts and API calls to the target cloud programming environment. The architecture supporting this methodology is composed of four components: the Algorithmic COncept Recognizer, which recognizes algorithmic concepts in the code, the API Ontology Builder, which extracts the graph by parsing source code and produces an ontology graph applying graph transformation patterns, the Schema Matcher which performs the matching among graphs and finally the Annotator which allows the user to semantically annotate the target API with concepts from the functional ontology. This work represents a contribute to facilitate software development in cloud scenario, since in cloud computing environment there are many APIs and services offered by different providers and big efforts are needed both to port applications in the cloud and to migrate from one provider to another. Future work planned includes the introduction of reasoning to extract additional knowledge based on inferential rules running on the acquired knowledge base and on optimization of the adopted graph matching algorithms for the specific graph representations of API components. Natural Language Processing techniques for ontology extraction, already developed by one of the authors [19], [20] are planned to be integrated, in order to deal with entire software artifacts which include natural language components (specification requirements, documentation, etc.).

Acknowledgements. The research leading to these results has received funding from the European Community's Seventh Framework Programme (FP7/2007-2013) under grant agreement n 256910 (mOSAIC Project), and by the Italian Ministry of University and Research, PRIN programme (project Cloud@Home). We would like to thank Manuela Serrao (Second University of Naples) who has implemented part of the Matchmaking algorithms.

References

1. Ratiu, D., Feilkas, M., Jurjens, J.: Extracting Domain Ontologies from Domain Specific APIs. In: Proc. of the 12th European Conf. on Software Maintenance and Reengineering, pp. 203–212. IEEE Computer Society (2008)
2. Zhang, Y., Rilling, J., Haarslev, V.: An Ontology-Based Approach to Software Comprehension - Reasoning about Security Concerns. In: 30th Annual International Computer Software and Applications Conference, COMPSAC 2006, vol. 1, pp. 333–342 (2006)
3. Alnusair, A., Zhao, T., Bodden, E.: Effective API navigation and reuse. In: Information Reuse and Integration, IEEE IRI, pp. 7–12 (2010)
4. Eberhart, A., Argawal, S.: SmartAPI - Associating Ontologies and APIs for Rapid Application Development. In: Ontologien in der und für die Softwaretechnik Workshop Anlsslich der Modellierung 2004. Marburg/Lahn (2004)
5. Bontcheva, K., Sabou, M.: Learning Ontologies from Software Artifacts: Exploring and Combining Multiple Sources. In: Workshop on Semantic Web Enabled Software Engineering, GA, USA (2006)
6. Na, H.-S., Choi, O.-H., Lim, J.-E.: A Metamodel-Based Approach for Extracting Ontological Semantics from UML Models. In: Aberer, K., Peng, Z., Rundensteiner, E.A., Zhang, Y., Li, X. (eds.) WISE 2006. LNCS, vol. 4255, pp. 411–422. Springer, Heidelberg (2006)
7. Na, H.S., Choi, O.H., Lim, J.E.: A Method for Building Domain Ontologies based on the Transformation of UML Models. In: Fourth International Conference on Software Engineering Research, Management and Applications, August 9-11, pp. 332–338 (2006)

8. Aho, A.V., Hopcroft, J.E., Ullman, J.D.: Data Structures and Algorithms. Addison-Wesley (1983)
9. Gamma, E., Helm, R., Johnson, R., Vlissides, J.: Design Patterns: Elements of Reusable Object-oriented Software. Addison-Wesley, Reading (1995)
10. Di Martino, B.: Algorithmic Concept Recognition to support High Performance Code Reengineering. Special Issue on Hardware/Software Support for High Performance Scientific and Engineering Computing of IEICE Transaction on Information and Systems E87-D(7), 1743–1750 (2004)
11. Di Martino, B., Kessler, C.W.: Two Program Comprehension Tools for Automatic Parallelization. IEEE Concurrency 8(1), 37–47 (2000)
12. Di Martino, B., Zima, H.P.: Support of Automatic Parallelization With Concept Comprehension. Journal of Systems Architecture 45(6-7), 427–439 (1999)
13. Knuth, D.E.: Semantics of context-free languages. Math. Syst. Theory 2(2), 127–145 (1968)
14. Di Martino, B.: Semantic Web Services Discovery based on Structural Ontology Matching. International Journal of Web and Grid Services (IJWGS) 5(1), 46–65 (2009)
15. Do, H.H., Rahm, E.: COMA: System for Flexible Combination of Schema Matching Approach. In: VLDB (2002)
16. Cordella, L.P., Foggia, P., Sansone, C., Vento, M.: Performance evaluation of the VF graph matching algorithm. In: Proc. of the 10th ICIAP, pp. 1172–1177. IEEE Computer Society Press (1999)
17. Gilleland, M.: Levenshtein Distance algorithm, Merriam Park Software (2000), http://www.merriampark.com/ld.html
18. Princeton University. Wordnet a lexical database for the English language (2006), http://wordnet.princeton.edu
19. Di Martino, B.: An Approach to Semantic Information Retrieval based on Natural Language Query Understanding. In: Daniel, F., Facca, F.M. (eds.) ICWE 2010. LNCS, vol. 6385, pp. 211–222. Springer, Heidelberg (2010)
20. Di Martino, B.: Ontology Querying and Matching for Semantic Based Retrieval of Semantically Annotated Documents. In: Proc. of IADIS International Conference on Applied Computing, Rome, November 19-21, pp. 227–232 (2009) ISBN 978-972-8924-97-3

Machine Learning for Emergent Middleware

Amel Bennaceur[1], Valérie Issarny[1], Daniel Sykes[1],
Falk Howar[2], Malte Isberner[2], Bernhard Steffen[2],
Richard Johansson[3], and Alessandro Moschitti[3]

[1] Inria, Paris-Rocquencourt, France
[2] Technical University of Dortmund, Germany
[3] University of Trento, Italy

Abstract. Highly dynamic and heterogeneous distributed systems
are challenging today's middleware technologies. Existing middleware
paradigms are unable to deliver on their most central promise, which
is offering interoperability. In this paper, we argue for the need to dynamically synthesise distributed system infrastructures according to the
current operating environment, thereby generating "Emergent Middleware" to mediate interactions among heterogeneous networked systems
that interact in an *ad hoc* way. The paper outlines the overall architecture of Enablers underlying Emergent Middleware, and in particular
focuses on the key role of learning in supporting such a process, spanning
statistical learning to infer the semantics of networked system functions
and automata learning to extract the related behaviours of networked
systems.

Keywords: Machine learning, Natural language processing, Automata
learning, Interoperability, Automated Mediation.

1 Introduction

Interoperability is a fundamental property in distributed systems, referring to
the ability for two or more systems, potentially developed by different manufac-
turers, to work together. Interoperability has always been a challenging problem
in distributed systems, and one that has been tackled in the past through a combination of middleware technologies and associated bridging solutions. However,
the scope and level of ambition of distributed systems continue to expand and
we now see a significant rise in complexity in the services and applications that
we seek to support.

Extreme distributed systems challenge the middleware paradigm that needs
to face on-the-fly connection of highly heterogeneous systems that have been
developed and deployed independently of each other. In previous work, we have
introduced the concept of *Emergent Middleware* to tackle the extreme levels of
heterogeneity and dynamism foreseen for tomorrow's distributed systems [13,4].

Emergent Middleware is an approach whereby the necessary middleware to
achieve interoperability is not a static entity but rather is generated dynamically
as required by the current context. This provides a very different perspective on

A. Moschitti and B. Plank (Eds.): EternalS 2013, CCIS 379, pp. 16–29, 2013.

middleware engineering and, in particular requires an approach that create and maintain the models of the current networked systems and exploit them to reason about the interaction of these networked systems and synthesise the appropriate artefact, i.e., the emergent middleware, that enable them to interoperate. However, although the specification of system capabilities and behaviours have been acknowledged as fundamental elements of system composition in open networks (especially in the context of the Web [8,16]), it is rather the exception than the norm to have such rich system descriptions available on the network.

This paper focuses on the pivotal role of learning technologies in supporting Emergent Middleware, including in building the necessary semantic run-time models to support the synthesis process and also in dealing with dynamism by constantly re-evaluating the current environment and context. While learning technologies have been deployed effectively in a range of domains, including in Robotics [26], Natural Language Processing [20], Software Categorisation [25], Model-checking [22], Testing [12], and Interface Synthesis [2], and Web service matchmaking [15], this is the first attempt to apply learning technologies in middleware addressing the core problem of interoperability.

This work is part of a greater effort within the CONNECT project[1] on the synthesis of Emergent Middleware for GMES-based systems that are representative of Systems of Systems. GMES[2] (Global Monitoring for Environment and Security) is the European Programme for the establishment of a European capacity for Earth Observation started in 1998. The services provided by GMES address six main thematic areas: land monitoring, marine environment monitoring, atmosphere monitoring, emergency management, security and climate change. The emergency management service directs efforts towards a wide range of emergency situations; in particular, it covers different catastrophic circumstances: Floods, Forest fires, Landslides, Earthquakes and volcanic eruptions, Humanitarian crises.

For our experiments, we concentrate on joint forest-fire operation that involves different European organisations due to, e.g., the cross-boarder location or criticality of the fire. The target GMES system involves highly heterogeneous NSs, which are connected on the fly as mobile NSs join the scene. Emergent Middleware then need to be synthesised to support such connections when they occur. In the following, we more specifically concentrate on the connection with the Weather Station NS, which may have various concrete instances, ranging from mobile stations to Internet-connected weather service. In addition, Weather Station NSs may be accessed from heterogeneous NSs, including mobile handheld devices of the various people on site and Command and Control —C2— centres (see Figure 1). We show how the learning techniques can serve complementing the base interface description of the NS with appropriate functional and behavioural semantics. It is in particular shown that the process may be fully automated, which is a key requirement of the Emergent Middleware concept.

---

[1] http://connect-forever.eu/

[2] http://www.gmes.info

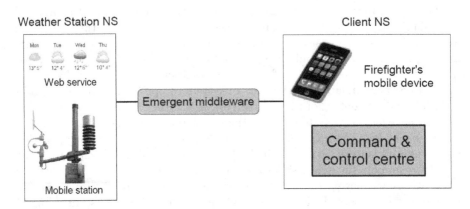

Fig. 1. Heterogeneous Connections with Weather Station NSs

2   Emergent Middleware

Emergent Middleware is synthesised in order to overcome the interoperability issue arising from two independently-developed Networked Systems (NSs). Given two Networked Systems where one implements the functionality required by the other, an Emergent Middleware that mediates application- and middleware-layer protocols implemented by the two NSs is deployed in the networked environment, based on the run-time models of the two NSs and provided that a protocol mediator can indeed be computed. The following section defines the NS model we use to represent the networked systems and reason about their interoperation. Then we present the by *Enablers*, i.e., active software entities that collaborate to realise the Emergent Middleware ensuring their interoperation.

2.1   Networked System Model

The definition of NS models takes inspiration from system models elaborated by the Semantic Web community toward application-layer interoperability. As depicted on Figure 2.(a), the NS model then decomposes into:

- *Interface*: The NS interface provides a microscopic view of the system by specifying fine-grained *actions* (or methods) that can be performed by (i.e., external action required by NS in the environment for proper functioning) and on (i.e., actions provided by the given NS in the networked environment) NS.
  There exist many interface definition languages and actually as many languages as middleware solutions. In our approach, we use a SAWSDL-like[3] XML schema. In particular, a major requirement is for interfaces to be annotated with ontology concepts so that the semantics of embedded actions and related parameters can be reasoned about.

---

[3] http://www.w3.org/2002/ws/sawsdl/spec/

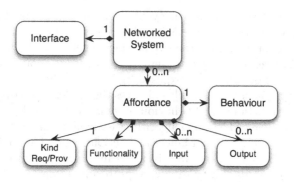

Fig. 2. The Networked System (NS) Model

- *Affordances*: The affordances (*a.k.a. capabilities* in OWL-S [16]) describe the high-level roles an NS plays, e.g., weather station, which are implemented as protocols over the system's observable actions (i.e., actions specified in the NS interface). The specification of an affordance decomposes into:
  - The *ontology-based semantic characterisation* of the high level *Functionality* implemented by the affordance, which is given in terms of the ontology concepts defining the given functionality and of the associated *Input* and *Output*. An affordance is further either *requested* or *provided* by the NS in the networked environment. In the former case, the NS needs to access a remote NS providing the affordance for correct operation; in the latter, the NS may be accessed for the implementation of the given affordance by a remote NS.
  - The affordance's *behaviour* describes how the actions of the interface are co-ordinated to achieve the system's given affordance. Precisely, the affordance behaviour is specified as a process over actions defined in the interface, and is represented as a Labelled Transition System (LTS).

2.2 Emergent Middleware Enablers

In order to produce an Emergent Middleware solution, an architecture of Enablers is required that executes the Emergent Middleware lifecycle. An Enabler is a software component that executes a phase of the Emergent Middleware, co-ordinating with other Enablers during the process.

The Emergent Middleware Enablers are informed by *domain ontologies* that formalise the concepts associated with the application domains (i.e., the vocabulary of the application domains and their relationship) of interest. Three challenging *Enablers* must then be comprehensively elaborated to fully realise Emergent Middleware:

1. The *Discovery Enabler* is in charge of discovering the NSs operating in a given environment. The *Discovery Enabler* receives both the advertisement messages and lookup request messages that are sent within the network

environment by the NSs using legacy discovery protocols (e.g., SLP[4]) thereby allowing the extraction of basic NS models based on the information exposed by NSs, i.e., identification of the NS interface together with middleware used for remote interactions. However, semantic knowledge about the NS must be learned as it is not commonly exposed by NSs directly.

2. The *Learning Enabler* specifically enhances the model of discovered NSs with the necessary functional and behavioural semantic knowledge. The *Learning Enabler* uses advanced learning algorithms to dynamically infer the ontology-based semantics of NSs' affordances and actions, as well as to determine the interaction behaviour of an NS, given the interface description exposed by the NS though some legacy discovery protocol. As detailed in subsequent sections, the Learning Enabler implements both statistical and automata learning to feed NS models with adequate semantic knowledge, i.e., functional and behavioural semantics.

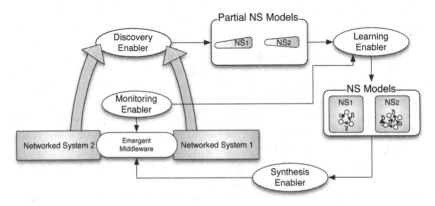

Fig. 3. The Enablers supporting Emergent Middleware

3. The *Synthesis Enabler* dynamically generates the software (i.e., Emergent Middleware) that mediates interactions between two legacy NS protocols to allow them to interoperate. In more detail, once NS models are complete, initial semantic matching of two affordances, that are respectively provided and required by two given NSs, may be performed to determine whether the two NSs are candidates to have an Emergent Middleware generated between them. The semantic matching of affordances is based on the subsumption relationship possibly holding between the concepts defining the functional semantics of the compared affordances.

   Given a functional semantic match of two affordances, the affordances' behaviour may be further analysed to ultimately generate a mediator in case of behavioural mismatch. It is the role of the *Synthesis Enabler* to analyse the behaviour of the two affordances and then synthesise—if applicable—the mediator component that is employed by the Emergent Middleware to enable the NSs to coordinate properly to realise the given affordance. For this,

---

[4] http://www.openslp.org/

the Synthesis Enabler performs automated behavioural matching and mapping of the two models. This uses the ontology-based semantics of actions to say where two sequences of actions in the two behaviours are semantically equivalent; based upon this, the matching and mapping algorithms determine a LTS model that represents the mediator. In few words, for both affordance protocols, the mediator LTS defines the sequences of actions that serve to translate actions from one protocol to the other, further including the possible re-ordering of actions.

The Learning phase is a continuous process where the knowledge about NSs is enriched over time, thereby implying that Emergent Middleware possibly needs to adapt as the knowledge evolves. In particular, the synthesised Emergent Middleware is equipped with monitoring probes that gather information on actual interaction between connected systems. This observed *Monitoring Data* is delivered to the Learning Enabler, where the learned hypotheses about the NSs' behaviour are compared to the observed interactions. Whenever an observation is made by the monitoring probes that is not contained in the learned behavioural models, another iteration of learning is triggered, yielding refined behavioural models. These models are then used to synthesise and deploy an evolved Emergent Middleware.

3   Machine Learning: A Brief Taxonomy

Machine learning is the discipline that studies methods for automatically inducing functions (or system of functions) from data. This broad definition of course covers an endless variety of subproblems, ranging from the least-squares linear regression methods typically taught at undergraduate level [20] to advanced structured output methods that learn to associate complex objects in the input [18] with objects in the output [14] or methods that infer whole computational structures [10]. To better understand the broad range of machine learning, one must first understand the conceptual differences between learning setups in terms of their prerequisites:

- *Supervised learning* is the most archetypical problem setting in machine learning. In this setting, the learning mechanism is provided with a (typically finite) set of labelled examples: a set of pairs $T = \{(x, y)\}$. The goal is to make use of the example set T to induce a function f, such that $f(x) = y$, for future unseen instances of (x, y) pairs (see for example [20]). A major hurdle in applying supervised learning is the often enormous effort of labelling the examples.
- *Unsupervised learning* lowers the entry hurdle for application by requiring only unlabelled example sets, i.e., $T = \{x\}$. In order to be able to come up with anything useful when no supervision is provided, the learning mechanism needs a bias that guides the learning process. The most well-known example of unsupervised learning is probably k-means clustering, where the learner learns to categorise objects into broad categories even though the

categories were not given a priori. Obviously, the results of unsupervised learning cannot compete with those of supervised learning.

- *Semi-supervised learning* is a pragmatic compromise. It allows one to use a combination of a small labelled example set $T_s = \{(x, y)\}$ together with a larger unlabelled example set $T_u = \{x\}$ in order to improve on both the plain supervised learner making use of T_s only and the unsupervised learner using all available examples.
- *Active learning* puts the supervisor in a feedback loop: whenever the (active) learner detects a situation where the available test set is inconclusive, the learner actively constructs complementing examples and asks the supervisor for the corresponding labelling. This learning discipline allows a much more targeted learning process, since the active learner can focus on the important/difficult cases (see for example [5]). The more structured the intended learning output is, the more successful active learning will be, as the required structural constraints are a good guide for the active construction of examples [3]. It has been successfully used in practice for inferring computational models via testing [11,10].

Learning technology has applicability in many domains. The next sections concentrate on the learning-based techniques that we are developing to enable the automated inference of semantic knowledge about Networked Systems, both functional and behavioural. The former relies on *statistical learning* while the latter is based on *automata learning*.

4   Statistical Learning for Inferring NS Functional Semantics

As discussed in Section 2.2, the first step in deciding whether two NSs will be able to interoperate consists in checking the compatibility of their *affordances* based on their functional semantics (i.e., ontology concepts characterising the purpose of the affordance). Then, in the successful cases, behavioural matching is performed so as to synthesise required mediator. This process highlights the central role of the functional matching of affordances in reducing the overall computation by acting as a kind of filter for the subsequent behavioural matching. Unfortunately, legacy applications do not normally provide affordance descriptions. We must therefore rely upon an engineer to provide them manually, or find some automated means to extract the probable affordance from the interface description. Note that it is not strictly necessary to have an absolutely correct affordance since falsely-identified matches will be caught in the subsequent detailed checks.

Since the interface is typically described by textual documentation, e.g., XML documents, we can capitalise on the long tradition of research in *text categorisation*. This studies approaches for automatically enriching text documents with semantic information. The latter is typically expressed by topic categories: thus text categorisation proposes methods to assign documents (in our case, interface descriptions) to one or more categories. The main tool for implementing modern systems for automatic document classification is machine learning based on vector space document representations.

In order to be able to apply standard machine learning methods for building categorizers, we need to represent the objects we want to classify by extracting informative *features*. Such features are used as indications that an object belongs to a certain category. For categorisation of documents, the standard representation of features maps every document into a vector space using the *bag-of-words* approach [24]. In this method, every word in the vocabulary is associated with a dimension of the vector space, allowing the document to be mapped into the vector space simply by computing the occurrence frequencies of each word. For example, a document consisting of the string "get Weather, get Station" could be represented as the vector $(2, 1, 1, \ldots)$ where, e.g., 2 in the first dimension is the frequency of the "get" token. The bag-of-words representation is considered the standard representation underlying most document classification approaches. In contrast, attempts to incorporate more complex structural information have mostly been unsuccessful for the task of categorisation of single documents [21] although they have been successful for complex relational classification tasks [19].

However, the task of classifying interface descriptions is different from classifying raw textual documents. Indeed, the interface descriptions are *semi-structured* rather than unstructured, and the representation method clearly needs to take this fact into account, for instance, by separating the vector space representation into regions for the respective parts of the interface description. In addition to the text, various semi-structured identifiers should be included in the feature representation, e.g., the names of the method and input parameters defined by the interface. The inclusion of identifiers is important since: (i) the textual content of the identifiers is often highly informative of the functionality provided by the respective methods; and (ii) the free text documentation is not mandatory and may not always be present.

For example, if the functionality of the interface are described by an XML file written in WSDL, we would have tags and structures, as illustrated by the text fragment below, which relates to a NS implementing a weather station and is part of the GMES scenario detailed in the next section on experiments:

```
<wsdl:message name="GetWeatherByZipCodeSoapIn">
    <wsdl:part name="parameters"
        element="tns:GetWeatherByZipCode" />
</wsdl:message>
 <wsdl:message name="GetWeatherByZipCodeSoapOut">
    <wsdl:part name="parameters"
        element="tns:GetWeatherByZipCodeResponse"/>
</wsdl:message>
```

It is clear that splitting the CamelCase identifier `GetWeatherStation` into the tokens `get`, `weather`, and `station`, would provide more meaningful and generalised concepts, which the learning algorithm can use as features. Indeed, to extract useful word tokens from the identifiers, we split them into pieces based on the presence of underscores or CamelCase; all tokens are then normalised to lowercase.

Once the feature representation is available, we use it to learn several classifiers, each of them specialised to recognise if the WSDL expresses some target semantic properties. The latter can also be concepts of an ontology. Consequently, our algorithm may be used to learn classifiers that automatically assign ontology concepts to actions defined in NS interfaces. Of course, the additional use of domain (but at the same time general) ontologies facilitates the learning process by providing effective features for the interface representation. In other words, WSDL, domain ontologies and any other information contribute to defining the vector representation used for training the concept classifiers.

5 Automata Learning for Inferring NS Behavioural Semantics

Automata learning can be considered as a key technology for dealing with *black box* systems, i.e., systems that can be observed, but for which no or little knowledge about the internal structure or even their intent is available. Active Learning (*a.k.a* regular extrapolation) attempts to construct a deterministic finite automaton that matches the behaviour of a given target system on the basis of test-based interaction with the system. The popular L^* algorithm infers Deterministic Finite Automata (DFAs) by means of *membership queries* that test whether certain strings (potential runs) are contained in the target system's language (its set of runs), and *equivalence queries* that compare intermediately constructed hypothesis automata for language equivalence with the target system.

In its basic form, L^* starts with a hypothesis automaton that treats all sequences of considered input actions alike, i.e., it has one single state, and refines this automaton on the basis of query results, iterating two main steps: (1) refining intermediate hypothesis automata using membership queries until a certain level of "consistency" is achieved (*test-based modelling*), and (2) testing hypothesis automata for equivalence with the target system via equivalence queries (*model-based testing*). This procedure successively produces state-minimal deterministic (hypothesis) automata consistent with all the encountered query results [3]. This basic pattern has been extended beyond the domain of learning DFAs to classes of automata better suited for modelling reactive systems in practice. On the basis of active learning algorithms for Mealy machines, inference algorithms for I/O-automata [1], timed automata [7], Petri Nets [6], and Register Automata [10], i.e., restricted flow graphs, have been developed.

While usually models produced by active learning are used in model-based verification or some other domain that requires complete models of the system under test (e.g., to prove absence of faults), here the inferred models serve as a basis for the interaction with the system for Emergent Middleware synthesis. This special focus poses unique requirements on the inferred models (discussed in detail in [9]), which become apparent in the following prototypical example.

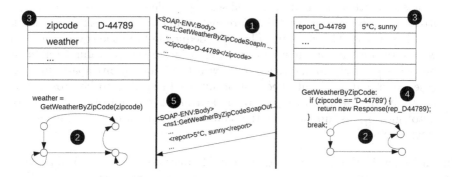

Fig. 4. Communicating Components

Figure 4 shows a typical interoperability scenario where two NSs are actual implementations of their specified interfaces. The NS on the right implements a weather service that provides weather forecasts for regions identified by ZIP codes. The NS on the left is a matching client. The two NSs communicate via SOAP protocol messages (1), (5), and together realise some protocol, which comprises a control part (2), and a data part (3) at both NSs. The data parts may be best described as a set of local variables or registers. The control part can be modelled as a labeled transition system with actual blocks of code labelling the transitions (4). Each code block of Fig. 4 would consist of an entry point for one interface method (e.g., `GetWeatherByZipCode`), conditions over parameters and local variables (e.g., comparing ZIP codes), assignments and operations on local variables (e.g., storing returned weather data), and a return statement.

To infer the behaviour of one NS (say, the right one from Fig. 4), the role of the other NS has to be undertaken by a learning algorithm, which is aware of the interface alphabet of the NS whose affordance's behaviour is to be learned. This interface alphabet is derived automatically from the interface description of the NS under scrutiny. A test-driver is then instantiated by the Learning Enabler, translating the alphabet symbols to remote invocations of the NS to be learned.

Now, to capture the interaction of the two NSs faithfully, two phenomena have to be made explicit in the inferred models:

- *Preconditions of Primitives:* Usually real systems operate on communication primitives that contain data values relevant to the communication context and have a direct impact on the exposed behaviour. Consider as an example session identifiers or sequence numbers that are negotiated between the communication participants and included in every message. The models have to make explicit causal relations between data parameters that are used in the communication (e.g, the exact session identifier that is returned when opening a new session has to be used in subsequent calls).
- *Effects of Primitives:* The learned models will only be useful for Emergent Middleware (mediator) synthesis within a given semantic context. Most NSs have well-defined purposes as characterised by affordances (e.g., getting

localised weather information). A subset of the offered communication primitives, when certain preconditions are met, will lead to successful conclusion of this purpose. This usually will not be deducible from the communication with a system: an automata learning algorithm in general cannot tell error messages and regular messages (e.g., weather information) apart. In such cases, information about effects of primitives rather has to be provided as an additional (semantic) input to the learning algorithm (e.g., in terms of ontologies [4]), as supported by the semantically annotated interface descriptions of NSes.

Summarizing, in the context of Emergent Middleware, especially dealing with parameters and value domains, and providing semantic information on the effect of communication primitives, are aspects that have to be addressed with care. We have reaffirmed this analysis in a series of experiments on actual implementations of NSs.

The automata learning technique is provided by LearnLib [17,23], a component-based framework for automata learning. In the produced model, each transition consists of two parts, separated by a forward-slash symbol: on the left

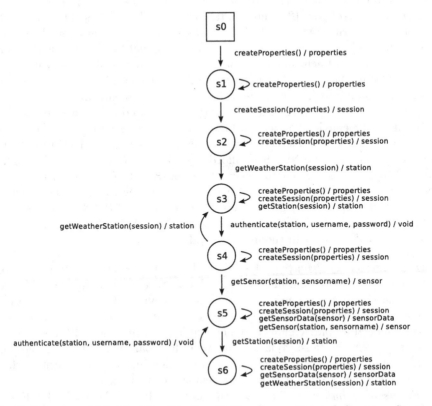

Fig. 5. Behavioural Model of the Weather Station Sensor Network Service – Starting State is s0

hand side an abstract parameterised symbol is denoted, while on the right hand side the named variable storing the invocation result is specified. Figure 5 depicts the behavioural description of the weather station, which was learned in 31 seconds on a portable computer, using 258 MQs.

The model correctly reflects the steps necessary, e.g., to read sensor data: `createProperties`, `createSession`, `getWeatherStation`, `authenticate` and `getSensor` have to be invoked before `getSensorData` can be called successfully. Additionally, the actual realisation of authentication, which cannot be deduced from the interface specification alone, is revealed in the inferred model. When simply looking at the parameter types, the action `getSensor` should be invocable directly after the `getWeatherStation` primitive. However, in reality `getSensor` is guarded by an authentication mechanism, meaning that `authenticate` has to be successfully invoked beforehand. Also, from the model, it is easily deducible that the `authenticate` action will indeed merely affect the provided station data object (and not, e.g., the whole session): requesting a new station data object will always necessitate another authentication step before `getSensor` can be invoked again, as that action requires an authenticated station data object.

6   Conclusion

This paper has presented the central role of learning in supporting the concept of Emergent Middleware, which revisits the middleware paradigm to sustain interoperability in increasingly heterogeneous and dynamic complex distributed systems. The production of Emergent Middleware raises numerous challenges, among which dealing with the *a priori* minimal knowledge about networked systems that is available to the generation process. Indeed, semantic knowledge about the interaction protocols run by the Networked Systems is needed to be able to reason and compose protocols in a way that enable NSs to collaborate properly. While making such knowledge available is increasingly common in Internet-worked environments (e.g., see effort in the Web service domain), it remains absent from the vast majority of descriptions exposed for the Networked Systems that are made available over the Internet. This paper has specifically outlined how powerful learning techniques that are being developed by the scientific community can be successfully applied to the Emergent Middleware context, thereby enabling the automated learning of both functional and behavioural semantics of NSs. In more detail, this paper has detailed how statistical and automata learning can be exploited to enable on-the-fly inference of functional and behavioural semantics of NSs, respectively.

Our experiments so far show great promise with respect to the effectiveness and efficiency of machine learning techniques applied to realistic distributed systems such as in the GMES case. Our short-term future work focuses on the fine tuning of machine learning algorithms according to the specifics of the networked systems as well as enhancing the learnt models with data representations and non-functional properties, which can result in considerable gains in terms of accuracy and performance. In the mid-term, we will work on the realisation of a continuous feedback loop from real-execution observations of the networked systems to update the learnt models dynamically as new knowledge becomes available and to improve the synthesised emergent middleware accordingly.

Acknowledgments. This research has been supported by the EU FP7 projects: CONNECT – Emergent Connectors for Eternal Software Intensive Networking Systems (project number FP7 231167), EternalS – "Trustworthy Eternal Systems via Evolving Software, Data and Knowledge" (project number FP7 247758) and by the EC Project, LiMoSINe – Linguistically Motivated Semantic aggregation engiNes (project number FP7 288024).

References

1. Aarts, F., Vaandrager, F.: Learning I/O Automata. In: Gastin, P., Laroussinie, F. (eds.) CONCUR 2010. LNCS, vol. 6269, pp. 71–85. Springer, Heidelberg (2010), http://dx.doi.org/10.1007/978-3-642-15375-4_6
2. Alur, R., Cerny, P., Madhusudan, P., Nam, W.: Synthesis of interface specifications for Java classes. In: Proc. POPL 2005 (2005)
3. Angluin, D.: Learning regular sets from queries and counterexamples. Inf. Comput. 75(2), 87–106 (1987)
4. Blair, G.S., Bennaceur, A., Georgantas, N., Grace, P., Issarny, V., Nundloll, V., Paolucci, M.: The Role of Ontologies in Emergent Middleware: Supporting Interoperability in Complex Distributed Systems. In: Kon, F., Kermarrec, A.-M. (eds.) Middleware 2011. LNCS, vol. 7049, pp. 410–430. Springer, Heidelberg (2011)
5. Cohn, D.A., Ghahramani, Z., Jordan, M.I.: Active learning with statistical models. J. Artif. Intell. Res. (JAIR) 4, 129–145 (1996)
6. Esparza, J., Leucker, M., Schlund, M.: Learning workflow petri nets 113, 205–228 (2011)
7. Grinchtein, O., Jonsson, B., Pettersson, P.: Inference of Event-Recording Automata Using Timed Decision Trees. In: Baier, C., Hermanns, H. (eds.) CONCUR 2006. LNCS, vol. 4137, pp. 435–449. Springer, Heidelberg (2006)
8. Heß, A., Kushmerick, N.: Learning to attach semantic metadata to web services. In: Fensel, D., Sycara, K., Mylopoulos, J. (eds.) ISWC 2003. LNCS, vol. 2870, pp. 258–273. Springer, Heidelberg (2003)
9. Howar, F., Jonsson, B., Merten, M., Steffen, B., Cassel, S.: On handling data in automata learning - considerations from the connect perspective. In: Margaria, T., Steffen, B. (eds.) ISoLA 2010, Part II. LNCS, vol. 6416, pp. 221–235. Springer, Heidelberg (2010)
10. Howar, F., Steffen, B., Jonsson, B., Cassel, S.: Inferring canonical register automata. In: Kuncak, V., Rybalchenko, A. (eds.) VMCAI 2012. LNCS, vol. 7148, pp. 251–266. Springer, Heidelberg (2012)
11. Howar, F., Steffen, B., Merten, M.: Automata learning with automated alphabet abstraction refinement. In: Jhala, R., Schmidt, D. (eds.) VMCAI 2011. LNCS, vol. 6538, pp. 263–277. Springer, Heidelberg (2011)
12. Hungar, H., Margaria, T., Steffen, B.: Test-based model generation for legacy systems. In: Proceedings of the International Test Conference, ITC 2003, September 30-October 2, vol. 1, pp. 971–980 (2003)

13. Issarny, V., Steffen, B., Jonsson, B., Blair, G., Grace, P., Kwiatkowska, M., Calinescu, R., Inverardi, P., Tivoli, M., Bertolino, A., Sabetta, A.: CONNECT Challenges: Towards Emergent Connectors for Eternal Networked Systems. In: 14th IEEE International Conference on Engineering of Complex Computer Systems (2009)
14. Joachims, T., Hofmann, T., Yue, Y., Yu, C.N.J.: Predicting structured objects with support vector machines. Commun. ACM 52(11), 97–104 (2009)
15. Katakis, I., Meditskos, G., Tsoumakas, G., Bassiliades, N., Vlahavas, I.P.: On the combination of textual and semantic descriptions for automated semantic web service classification. In: Iliadis, L., Vlahavas, I., Bramer, M. (eds.) Artificial Intelligence Applications and Innovations III. IFIP, vol. 296, pp. 95–104. Springer, Boston (2009)
16. Martin, D.L., Burstein, M.H., McDermott, D.V., McIlraith, S.A., Paolucci, M., Sycara, K.P., McGuinness, D.L., Sirin, E., Srinivasan, N.: Bringing semantics to web services with OWL-S. In: World Wide Web, pp. 243–277 (2007)
17. Merten, M., Steffen, B., Howar, F., Margaria, T.: Next generation learnLib. In: Abdulla, P.A., Leino, K.R.M. (eds.) TACAS 2011. LNCS, vol. 6605, pp. 220–223. Springer, Heidelberg (2011)
18. Moschitti, A.: Efficient convolution kernels for dependency and constituent syntactic trees. In: Fürnkranz, J., Scheffer, T., Spiliopoulou, M. (eds.) ECML 2006. LNCS (LNAI), vol. 4212, pp. 318–329. Springer, Heidelberg (2006)
19. Moschitti, A.: Kernel methods, syntax and semantics for relational text categorization. In: Proceedings of ACM 17th Conference on Information and Knowledge Management, CIKM, Napa Valley, United States (2008)
20. Moschitti, A.: Kernel-based machines for abstract and easy modeling of automatic learning. In: Bernardo, M., Issarny, V. (eds.) SFM 2011. LNCS, vol. 6659, pp. 458–503. Springer, Heidelberg (2011)
21. Moschitti, A., Basili, R.: Complex linguistic features for text classification: A comprehensive study. In: McDonald, S., Tait, J.I. (eds.) ECIR 2004. LNCS, vol. 2997, pp. 181–196. Springer, Heidelberg (2004)
22. Peled, D., Vardi, M.Y., Yannakakis, M.: Black box checking. In: Wu, J., Chanson, S.T., Gao, Q. (eds.) Formal Methods for Protocol Engineering and Distributed Systems. IFIP AICT, vol. 28, pp. 225–240. Springer, Heidelberg (1999)
23. Raffelt, H., Steffen, B., Berg, T., Margaria, T.: LearnLib: a framework for extrapolating behavioral models. Int. J. Softw. Tools Technol. Transf. 11(5), 393–407 (2009)
24. Salton, G., Wong, A., Yang, C.S.: A vector space model for automatic indexing. Tech. Rep. TR74-218, Department of Computer Science, Cornell University, Ithaca, New York (1974)
25. Selby, R., Porter, A.: Learning from examples: generation and evaluation of decision trees for software resource analysis. IEEE Transactions on Software Engineering 14(12) (1988)
26. Stone, P., Veloso, M.: Multiagent systems: A survey from a machine learning perspective. Autonomous Robots 8 (2000)

Security Oracle Based on Tree Kernel Methods

Andrea Avancini and Mariano Ceccato

Fondazione Bruno Kessler
Trento, Italy

Abstract. The objective of software testing is to stress a program to reveal programming defects. Security testing is, more specifically, that branch of testing which aims to reveal defects that could lead to security problems. Most of security testing declensions, however, have been mostly interested in the automatic generation of test cases that "try" to reveal a vulnerability, rather than assessing if test cases have actually "managed" to expose security issues.

In this paper, we cope with the latter problem. We investigate on the feasibility of using tree kernel methods to implement a classifier able to evaluate if a test case revealed a vulnerability, i.e. a security oracle for injection attacks. We compare six different variants of tree kernel methods in terms of their effectiveness in detecting attacks.

1 Introduction

Among the programming defects that threat the reliability of web applications, those that concern security aspects are probably the most critical. In fact, vulnerabilities could be exploited by attackers to block the correct execution of a business service (denial of service) or to steal sensitive data, such as credit card numbers or medical records.

According to statistics on open source projects [4], one of the most severe class of vulnerabilities is Cross-site scripting (XSS for short). An XSS vulnerability is exploited when input values that contain malicious HTML or JavaScript code are printed in a web page. As result of the attack, the vulnerable page will contain the injected code and its content and/or behavior will be controlled by the attacker.

Security testing is a process intended to spot and verify security vulnerabilities, by showing an instance of input data that exposes the problem. A developer requested to fix a security defect may take advantage of a security test case to better understand the issue (vulnerabilities often involve complex mechanics) and to elaborate a patch. Eventually, a security test may be resorted to assess if a maintenance task has shown to be resolutive.

There is a number of approaches for security testing of web applications [18,12,13,9,8,11], which are mainly focused on the test case generation phase, while the problem of verifying if a test case actually exploits a vulnerability has given a marginal importance. In fact, checking if a test case has been able to exploit a vulnerability is either addressed by manual filtering [18] or in a way that

A. Moschitti and B. Plank (Eds.): EternalS 2013, CCIS 379, pp. 30–43, 2013.

is customized for a specific test case generation strategy. For example, in [12], verifying if a test case is a successful attack relies on the knowledge about the way the test case has been previously constructed, i.e. if the output page contains the same JavaScript fragment that has been used to generate the test case itself.

In the present paper we address the problem of developing a security oracle, a classifier able to detect when a vulnerability is exploited by a test case, i.e. verifying if a test case is an instance of a successful attack. Our oracle is meant to be independent from the approach deployed to generate test cases, so that it can be reused in many different contexts.

We propose to construct the oracle resorting to tree kernel methods. The classifier is trained on a set of test cases containing both safe executions and successful attacks. In fact, it is quite common for a software project to document past defects (including vulnerabilities) that have already been fixed. The oracle is then deployed when generating new security test cases, intended to spot new vulnerability problems.

The paper is organized as follows. Section 2 shows the background on web application vulnerabilities, required for presenting the security oracle in Section 3. Preliminary experimental results are presented in Section 4. Comparison with the state of the art (Sections 5) and conclusions (Section 6) close the paper.

2   Web Application Vulnerabilities

Cross-site scripting vulnerabilities are caused by improper or missing validation of input data (e.g., coming from the user). Input data may contain HTML fragments that, if appended to a web page, could alter the page final content such that malicious code is injected.

Figure 1 shows an example of dynamic web page that contains a vulnerability. The code between "<?PHP" and "?>" is interpreted by the web server as PHP[1] code and executed when the web page is processed. On incoming HTML requests, the web server executes the PHP code in the page, which handles input values and generates a textual output that represents the dynamic part of the requested page. On PHP termination, the web server sends the resulting output back to the requester web browser as an HTML response.

The example contains a reflected XSS vulnerability, i.e. there exists an execution flow along which the input value *param* is not adequately validated before being printed (*echo* statement in PHP) in the output page (line 15). Any code contained in this input value, if not properly validated, may be added to the current page and eventually executed.

The page accepts three parameters, *param*, *cardinality* and *op*, and adopts a quite common pattern, performing different actions according to the value of one of the parameters. In case the parameter *op* is set, the page will show a table, otherwise it will display a menu. The number of rows in the table and

---

[1] Even if the example is in PHP, the proposed approach is general and can be applied on web applications implemented in other programming languages.

```
       <html>
       <body>
       <?php
1      $p = $_GET['param'];
2      $n = $_GET['cardinality'];
3      $op = $_GET['op'];
4      if ( $n < 1 )              //input validation
5          die;
6      if ( strpos($p,'<script') !== false)
7          $p=htmlspecialchars($p);
8      if (isset($op)) {              //print table
9          echo '<table_border=1>';
10         for ($i=0; $i<$n; $i++) {
11             echo '<tr><td>first_cell_</td>' .
                   '<td>second_cell</td>' .
                   '<td>third_cell</td></tr>';
           }
12         echo "</table>";
       }
       else {                         //print menu
13         for ($i=0; $i<$n; $i++) {
14             echo '<a_href=first.php>link_#' .
               $i . '</a>';
           }
       }
15     echo $p;                       //vulnerability
       ?>
       </body>
       </html>
```

Fig. 1. Running example of a XSS vulnerability on PHP code

the number of links in the menu depend on the value of *cardinality*. Parameter *param* is just printed.

On lines 1–3, input values are read from the incoming HTML request (represented in PHP as the special associative array *$_GET*) and assigned to local variables *$p*, *$n* and *$op* respectively.

On lines 4–7, input values are validated. In case *$n* contains a value smaller than 1 or a string that does not represent a number, the execution aborts (die statement at line 5). At line 7, the value of variable *$p* is validated. Validation, however, is done only when condition on line 6 holds, which is not sufficient to cover all the possible dangerous cases. For example, harmful code containing a different tag (e.g. <a>) or with a space between < and script may skip the sanitization.

Depending on the value of variable *$op*, either a table (lines 8–12) or a menu (lines 13–14) is shown. Eventually, variable *$p* is printed at line 15 possibly causing a security threat, because of inadequate validation at lines 6–7.

An example of successful attack is represented by an HTML request containing the parameter *param* set to the subsequent JavaScript code:

```
<a href="" onclick="this.href= 'www.evil.com?data=
'%2Bdocument.cookie"> click here</a>
```

When such value is appended to the response page, it alters its HTML structure (%2B is decoded as "+"), injecting a brand new link "*click here*" (i.e., <a> tag) which points to an external web site controlled by the attacker (i.e., *www.evil.com*). In case such link is triggered by the legitimate user, his/her cookie is encoded as an HTML request parameter and sent to the attacker-controlled web site. With the stolen cookie, the attacker may pretend to impersonate the legitimate user.

The automatic generation of input values to test such a vulnerable page can be addressed in quite a cheap way by applying a number of different strategies. After input generation, however, output needs to be validated, i.e. a *security oracle* is required to check whether code injection has taken place. In the subsequent sections we present our approach to use kernel methods to implement a security oracle, i.e. to classify executions of dynamic web pages as safe executions or as successful code injections. In the latter case, a concrete vulnerability is detected.

3   Security Oracle

The goal of an XSS attack is to inject JavaScript or HTML code fragments into a web page. Thus, consequences of a successful injection should be evident as *structural* changes in the page under attack, when compared with the same page running under normal conditions.

Web applications, however, are highly dynamic and their structure or content may vary a lot, even without code injection. For instance, on the running example of Figure 1, the same PHP script under harmless conditions can display different results (number of table rows) and can take different alternative actions (showing a table or a menu).

A web page can be represented by the parse tree of the corresponding HTML code, thus injection of malicious code corresponds to a change in the parse tree with respect to the intended structure. Figure 2 shows the parse trees of three HTML outputs of the running example: Figure 2(a) and (b) show the parse trees of safe executions that contain, respectively, a table with three rows and a menu with tree links. Figure 2(c), instead, represents the parse tree of the same page under attack, a menu with two intended links and, in addition, a malicious link. By looking at Figure 2, we can observe that the intrinsic variability of safe executions (e.g., between (a) and (b)) can be wider than the variability due to code injection (e.g., between (b) and (c)). So, a similarity metric may not be adequate to detect successful attacks. The security oracle should distinguish between those variations that are safe due to the dynamic behavior of the application under test and those variations caused by code injection due to successful attacks. The classifier must be trained with instances of parse trees taken from both the

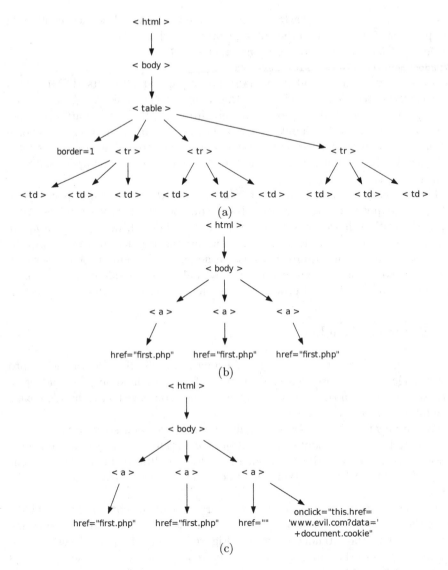

Fig. 2. Parse trees of output pages for the running example. Trees (a) and (b) represent safe executions. Tree (c) represents an injection attack.

classes of possible variations. Under these assumptions, the security oracle problem can be formulated as a binary classification problem, that can be addressed by relying on kernel methods. In particular, we deal with parse trees, so kernel methods that fit this problem definition better are *tree kernels* [5].

In constructing the oracle, first we need to run static analysis to get a list of potential vulnerabilities in a preparation step:

1. **Static analysis:** taint analysis is run to detect candidate vulnerabilities in the application under test. Each vulnerability defines a coverage criterion for security testing (i.e. goal of security testing is to cover a vulnerability).

At the end of the preliminary phase, the oracle can be constructed by performing the following steps:

1. **Test case generation:** safe (i.e. without injecting any code) test cases are generated, either manually or automatically, such that they cover the vulnerability criteria detected by static analysis. For this purpose, we reused a tool we developed in a previous work [2] but any test case generation approach is applicable in principle.
2. **Attack generation:** some test cases are turned into candidate attacks by adding selected attack strings, extracted from a library of malicious fragments of HTML and JavaScript, to input values. This library has been taken from a publicly available tool [17] for penetration testing and black-box fuzzing.
3. **Manual filtering:** test cases and candidate attacks are run on the web application under analysis. Results are manually classified as safe executions or successful injection attacks. The output pages are then parsed by using Txl [7] and the resulting HTML parse trees are stored.
4. **Training:** parse trees of successful attacks and safe executions are used respectively as *positive* and *negative* examples for the learning phase of the oracle.
5. **Classification:** the oracle is ready. To evaluate a new test case, the test must be executed on the application under analysis and the HTML output must be parsed. Eventually, the oracle relies on the kernel to classify the HTML parse tree either as safe execution or as successful attack. Classification is performed on those pages that contain a candidate vulnerability and for which some attacks have been successfully crafted.

3.1   Static Analysis

The identification of vulnerabilities relies on taint analysis [10], a static analysis technique that tracks the tainted/untainted status of variables throughout the application's control flow. A vulnerability is reported whenever a possibly tainted variable is used in a sink statement (e.g. print). In case of XSS [20], tainted values are those that come from untrusted sources (data base and user input) and sinks are all the print statements that append a value to the resulting web page. Tainted status is propagated on assignments and tainted variables become untainted upon sanitization (e.g., function *htmlspecialchars* in PHP). Taint analysis is formulated as a flow analysis [16] problem, where the information propagated in the control flow graph is the set of variables holding tainted values.

Taint analysis provides the *data dependency slice* that gives raise to a vulnerability. The data slice consists of the chain of assignments that contribute to make a tainted value flow to a sink statement, skipping validation routines. The data slice for the vulnerability shown in Figure 1 is composed by lines {1, 15}, because the variable $p is assigned the input data *param* at line 1 and it is printed later at line 15.

On top of this information, we also collect all those control statements that hold a control dependence on the statements in the data slices, since they are responsible to guide the execution along to or away from a vulnerable path. These statements are the branches to traverse in order to make a tainted value reach a sink statement, they are called *target branches*. Target branches for the example shown in Figure 1 are {4-6, 6-8}, where the former (4-6) is needed to avoid the termination of the script and the latter (6-8) to skip the sanitization of the variable $p at line 7 that would break the data slice and stop propagating the tainted value before reaching the sink statement.

Target branches represent a vulnerability coverage criterion for the security testing activity. A test exposes a vulnerability only when it makes the execution take all the corresponding target branches.

3.2   Test Case Generation

In order to generate test cases that satisfy the vulnerability criteria defined by static analysis, we rely on a tool we developed in previous works [1,2] that integrates heuristics (Genetic Algorithms) and analytic solutions (SMT solver). Many test case generation approaches, however, exist in the literature [18,12,13,9,8,11] and any of them is, in principle, applicable to this context. Alternatively, test cases can be also manually written, for example by translating the application use cases into test cases.

It could happen, however, that the test generation phase computes just few (or just one) test cases for each vulnerability criterion. More distinct test cases are needed to train the classifier with an appropriate level of generality. Then, to increase the number of total tests available, we mutate the initial set of test case(s) by using few mutation operators that have been previously implemented.

Since the focus of this paper is on the security oracle, we will not give more details of the test case generation part, and we will use the available tool as a black box. More details about this phase can be found in previous works [1,2].

3.3   Attack Generation

For turning security test cases into code injection exploits, attack strings are injected into test input data. Attack strings come from a library of fragments of typical attacks (e.g., HTML tags containing scripts and links) that have been already used in penetration testing and in black-box fuzzing [17]. When requested, an attack fragment is randomly chosen from the library and injected into one of the parameter values of an original test case. Then, the newly created candidate attack is executed to check if it still traverses all the *target branches*.

4   Empirical Results

Identification of candidate vulnerabilities has been performed by using Pixy [10], a publicly available tool for taint analysis of PHP code, which reports a list of candidate vulnerabilities derived from the source code of the application under test. A vulnerability is represented by a sequence of target branches to be executed, our vulnerability coverage criterion. A tool developed in previous works [1,2] is resorted to automatically generate an initial set of test cases that satisfies the coverage criteria.

The experimentation has been conducted using SVM-light-TK[2] version 1.5 as kernel machine. This tool extends SVM-light tool[3] with kernel support by implementing different kernel methods. The ones selected for the experiment are listed in the following:

- Standard (Tree) Kernel (SK) [5],
- Sub Tree Kernel (STK) [19],
- Subset Tree Kernel (SSTK) [6],
- Subset Tree Kernel (SSTK) with bag-of-words (BOW) feature [21],
- Partial Tree Kernel (PTK) [14],
- Partial Tree Kernel with no leaves (uPTK) [15].

4.1   Prototype Results

To understand the applicability of the proposed approach in a small and controllable context, we first tested it on a mock-up case study, a simple web application from which the running example of Figure 1 has been taken. The case study consists of a single PHP script of 37 lines of code which represents a typical pattern of a dynamic web page. It implements two different functionalities, according to the value of an input parameter (generating a table or a sequence of links). This script contains two XSS vulnerabilities.

A total of 3,470 test cases have been generated using previously developed tools [1,2]. These tests have been manually filtered to remove false positives. Among the remaining ones, we selected 460 safe executions and 46 code injection attacks, to respect a 1:10 proportion among the two classes[4]. This corpus of data has been randomly split into two parts, 50% for training and 50% for assessment. While splitting data, we took care of dividing attacks uniformly between the two parts.

Tuning of cost-factor value has been achieved with the following procedure. Initially, only the 80% of the training data (202 test cases, training set) has been used to build a preliminary model, while the remaining 20% (51 test cases, tuning set) has been used to tune the cost-factor. Then, the initial model has been adopted to classify the tuning set by iteratively changing the cost-factor value from 1 to 50. We selected the optimal cost-factor value as the one that

---

[2] http://disi.unitn.it/moschitti/Tree-Kernel.htm
[3] http://www.joachims.org/
[4] Generating attacks is usually harder than generating safe tests.

showed the best trade off between precision and recall in classifying the tuning data set, i.e. the configuration with the highest value of F-measure.

Eventually, the final model is constructed on all the training data (training set and tuning set), applying the optimal cost-factor value. After learning, performances of the final security oracle are measured on the assessment data set.

Table 1. Experimental results for mock-up application

Kernel	Optimal Cost-factor	Precision	Recall	F-measure
SK	1	100%	78%	88%
STK	20	7%	100%	13%
SSTK	1	100%	78%	88%
SSTK + BOW	1	100%	78%	88%
PTK	8	100%	17%	30%
uPTK	7	100%	39%	56%

Table 1 reports the results collected on the prototype script for the six different kernel methods introduced above. The first column contains the name of the kernel method, while the second column reports the optimal cost-factor value that has been chosen to run the experiment with the corresponding kernel. Third, fourth and fifth columns report respectively precision, recall and F-measure, obtained by running the classifier on the assessment data set.

The best results have been achieved by three methods, SK, SSTK and SSTK + BOW. By running these methods, reported precision and recall have been 100% and 78% respectively, meaning that all the test cases that have been classified as attacks (18) are real attacks, while 5 attacks have been classified as safe tests. After manual inspection, we discovered the reason for not obtaining 100% recall. Despite the attack library [17] contains several distinct HTML syntactic elements, we noticed that training data contained no instances of attacks with the same HTML syntactic structure used in the 5 misclassified attacks. Richer training data, containing at least one instance of any possible syntactic form of attacks, would have improved the performance of the oracle.

Among the other tree kernel methods, the best results have been obtained by uPTK. In this case, 9 attacks out of 23 have been classified in the correct way, achieving a high precision (100%) but a fairly low recall (39%). PTK method performed slightly worse, obtaining equal precision (100%) but even lower recall (17%). In fact, just 4 attacks have been correctly recognized by this method.

The remaining method, STK, reported the worst performance. When used, STK observed an unstable behavior with respect to different cost-factor values. For cost-factor values lower or equal than 8, all the objects in the data set are classified as safe test cases (100% precision and 0% recall) while, for values greater than 8, all the tests are classified as attacks (low precision and 100% recall).

4.2 Empirical Assessment

In order to evaluate the performance of the security oracle on regular web applications, we tested it on a real world case study written in PHP, Yapig version 0.95b. Yapig is an open source web application that implements an image gallery management system, allowing users to publish and comment pictures organized in galleries. It consists of 9,113 lines of code and 53 source files, with 160 user-defined functions and 2,638 branches.

Table 2. Test cases automatically generated for Yapig

Vulnerability	Generated test cases			Used test cases	
	Safe tests	Candidate attacks	Real attacks	Safe tests	Attacks
1_1	600	10	10	100	10
1_2	420	4	4	40	4
2_1	163	155	155	160	16
2_2	68	19	0	0	0
2_3	14	0	0	0	0
2_4	175	19	19	170	17
2_5	52	7	7	50	5
2_6	299	0	0	0	0
Total	1,791	214	195	520	52

At first, we generated test cases using our tool [1,2]. Data about test case generation are reported on Table 2. The first column reports the name of the vulnerability, where the syntax i_j is used to group together similar vulnerabilities. In fact, vulnerabilities with the same i insist on the same sink statement (e.g., the same *echo* statement), but having different sequences of target branches, i.e. different execution flows. All the vulnerabilities in Table 2 refer to *upload.php* page, which is responsible to handle the functionality of uploading pictures in Yapig. Users may select pictures from their local hard drive and upload them on the server by resorting to the capabilities offered by this page.

The second and third columns of Table 2 report respectively the number of safe test cases and candidate attacks that has been automatically generated. Eventually, the fourth column reports the number of real attacks that are still available after manual filtering. As in the previous experiment, the test cases have been selected to respect a 1:10 ratio between attacks and safe tests for each vulnerability (fifth and sixth column).

A total of 2,005 distinct test cases has been generated. 1,791 of them are safe by construction (no attack fragments have been injected), while 214 are candidate attacks. After manual inspecting them, real attacks resulted to be 195. 520 safe executions and 52 code injection attacks have been considered in total, 50% of them have been used for training and 50% for assessment. Tuning of cost-factor has been performed by using the same procedure described in Section 4.1. For two kernels (PTK and uPTK), two distinct configurations of the cost factor gave symmetrical results (high precision/low recall and vice versa), so we decided to keep both. We called PTK(p) and uPTK(p) the configurations with higher precision and PTK(r) and uPTK(r) those with higher recall.

After completing the learning phase, performances of the security oracle have been assessed on the assessment data set.

Table 3. Experimental results for Yapig

Kernel	Optimal Cost-factor	Precision	Recall	F-measure
SK	1	9%	100%	17%
STK	21	12%	100%	22%
SSTK	9	9%	100%	17%
SSTK + BOW	7	9%	100%	17%
PTK(p)	6	100%	27%	42%
PTK(r)	11	21%	100%	34%
uPTK(p)	4	100%	27%	42%
uPTK(r)	11	21%	100%	34%

Table 3 reports experimental results collected on Yapig for the 6 different kernel methods. The first column reports the kernel, the second column the optimal cost-factor value, while third, fourth and fifth columns report precision, recall and F-measure.

The best results in terms of F-measure (42%) have been achieved by two methods, PTK(p) and uPTK(p). By running these methods, reported precision and recall have been 100% and 27% respectively, meaning that all the test cases that have been classified as attacks (i.e., 7) are real attacks, while 19 attacks have been classified as safe tests, which represents a fairly bad result since the primary objective of the oracle should be not to miss attacks. Furthermore, any attack misclassification might have severe consequences in terms of security and should be avoided.

The other two variants of these same methods, PTK(r) and uPTK(r), registered the second best result with F-measure of 34%, low precision (21%) but high recall (100%). This result, despite the low precision that indicates the presence of false positives (100 out of 286 tests), is preferable in the domain of security testing since no false negatives have been found, i.e. no attacks have been misclassified as safe tests.

Among the remaining four kernel methods, the best results have been obtained by STK. All the attacks have been classified in the correct way, recording high recall (100%) but low precision (12%). SK, SSTK and SSTK + BOW methods performed slightly worse, obtaining equal recall (100%) but even lower precision (9%). In fact, all the tests in the assessment have been classified as attacks, generating 260 false alarms that would have required manual inspection by the developers.

The high recall on Yapig (100%) can be justified by the fact that, differently from the previous experiment, the training set is much more representative of the attacks. Safe tests are also well represented, since the PHP code tested is highly dynamic and could generate different HTML pages, according to which vulnerability data slice is tested. Vulnerability criteria, in fact, are represented by different sets of target branches that lead to the presence of a variety of HTML structures in the resulting page.

In terms of scalability, the security oracle showed to be able to work on real size code. HTML pages parsed by the oracle contain up to 1,202 distinct nodes, which represents a fairly complex HTML page with several syntactic elements.

5   Related Works

A fundamental problem of security testing is deciding about successful attacks, i.e. when a test case is able to inject malicious code and to reveal a defect. Initially, checking code injection was a manual task delegated to programmers. For instance, in the work by Tappenden et al. [18], security testing is approached with an agile methodology using HTTP-unit, while verification of test outcomes is a manual task.

Other approaches provide a higher level of automation. In [12], a library of documented attacks is used to generate valid inputs for a web application. A symbolic data base is implemented to propagate tainted status of input values through the data base to the final attack sinks. A first stage of the oracle adopts dynamic taint analysis to verify if tainted data are used in a sink, while a second stage performs a comparison of safe pages with pages generated by candidate attacks. This check consists in verifying if pages differ with respect to "script-inducing constructs", i.e. new scripts or different *href* attributes.

In other works [13,8], the oracle consists in checking if a response page contains the same *<script>* tag passed as input. McAllister et al. [13] adopt a black-box approach to detect XSS vulnerabilities. Data collected during the interaction with real users are subjected to fuzzing, so as to increase test coverage. The oracle for XSS attacks checks if the script passed as input is also present in the output page.

The paper by Halfond et al. [8] presents a complete approach to identify XSS and SQLI vulnerabilities in Java web applications. (1) Input vectors are identified and grouped together with their domains into input interfaces. Then (2), attack patterns are used to generate many attacks for these interfaces. Eventually (3), page execution is monitored and HTTP response is inspected to verify if attacks are successful. The oracle detects if the response page contains the same script tag that was injected in the input data.

Limiting the check to injected script tags guarantees a high precision, but recall may be low, because of vulnerabilities depending on other tags may not be detected by these oracles. Our approach is more general, because it relies on structural differences among safe executions and attacks, that are general enough to capture different forms of code injection.

To assess the classification accuracy of security oracle, we needed a corpus of safe test cases and successful attacks. To build this corpus, we conveniently relied on a previous tool developed by us in previous works [1,2], but other approaches for automatic generation of test cases are also applicable. However, the objective of this paper was not to evaluate the performances in test case generation, but the accuracy of the oracle in classifying tests.

This paper extends a preliminary workshop paper [3] that sketched the initial intuition of the security oracle.

6   Conclusion

In this paper, we used kernel methods for implementing a security oracle for web applications. The proposed security oracle has been assessed on a real PHP application, with good performances in terms of precision, recall and scalability. From this experiment, we learned which two kernel methods are the most appropriate to use in this domain, they are Partial Tree Kernel (PTK) and Partial Tree Kernel with no leaves (uPTK). Moreover, our empirical assessment highlighted an important aspect of the approach, attacks should be appropriately represented among learning data in order to improve the performance of the oracle.

As future works, we intend to experiment with customized kernel methods to improve the performance of the security oracle. Moreover, we plan to conduct studies with web applications written in other languages and, possibly, to consider different kind of vulnerabilities (e.g., Cross-site request forgery).

Acknowledgements. The research described in this paper has been partially supported by the European Community's Seventh Framework Programme (FP7/2007-2013) under the grants #247758: ETERNALS – Trustworthy Eternal Systems via Evolving Software, Data and Knowledge, and #288024: LiMoSINE – Linguistically Motivated Semantic aggregation engiNes.

References

1. Avancini, A., Ceccato, M.: Towards security testing with taint analysis and genetic algorithms. In: Proceedings of the 2010 ICSE Workshop on Software Engineering for Secure Systems, pp. 65–71. ACM (2010)
2. Avancini, A., Ceccato, M.: Security testing of web applications: A search-based approach for cross-site scripting vulnerabilities. In: 2011 11th IEEE International Working Conference on Source Code Analysis and Manipulation, SCAM, pp. 85–94. IEEE (2011)
3. Avancini, A., Ceccato, M.: Grammar based oracle for security testing of web applications. In: Proceedings of 7th International Workshop on Automation of Software Test (2012) (to appear)
4. Christey, S., Martin, R.A.: Vulnerability type distributions in cve. Tech. rep., The MITRE Corporation (2006),
   http://cwe.mitre.org/documents/vuln-trends/index.html
5. Collins, M., Duffy, N.: Convolution kernels for natural language. In: Advances in Neural Information Processing Systems 14, pp. 625–632. MIT Press (2001)

6. Collins, M., Duffy, N.: New ranking algorithms for parsing and tagging: kernels over discrete structures, and the voted perceptron. In: Proceedings of the 40th Annual Meeting on Association for Computational Linguistics, ACL 2002, pp. 263–270. Association for Computational Linguistics, Stroudsburg (2002), http://dx.doi.org/10.3115/1073083.1073128
7. Cordy, J.: The TXL source transformation language. Science of Computer Programming 61(3), 190–210 (2006)
8. Halfond, W.G.J., Choudhary, S.R., Orso, A.: Improving penetration testing through static and dynamic analysis. Software Testing, Verification and Reliability 21(3), 195–214 (2011)
9. Huang, Y.W., Tsai, C.H., Lee, D., Kuo, S.Y.: Non-detrimental web application security scanning. In: 15th International Symposium on Software Reliability Engineering, ISSRE 2004, pp. 219–230 (November 2004)
10. Jovanovic, N., Kruegel, C., Kirda, E.: Pixy: A static analysis tool for detecting web application vulnerabilities (short paper). In: SP 2006: Proceedings of the 2006 IEEE Symposium on Security and Privacy, pp. 258–263. IEEE Computer Society, Washington, DC (2006)
11. Kals, S., Kirda, E., Kruegel, C., Jovanovic, N.: Secubat: a web vulnerability scanner. In: Proceedings of the 15th International Conference on World Wide Web, WWW 2006, pp. 247–256. ACM, New York (2006)
12. Kieyzun, A., Guo, P., Jayaraman, K., Ernst, M.: Automatic creation of sql injection and cross-site scripting attacks. In: IEEE 31st International Conference on Software Engineering, ICSE 2009, pp. 199–209 (May 2009)
13. McAllister, S., Kirda, E., Kruegel, C.: Leveraging user interactions for in-depth testing of web applications. In: Lippmann, R., Kirda, E., Trachtenberg, A. (eds.) RAID 2008. LNCS, vol. 5230, pp. 191–210. Springer, Heidelberg (2008)
14. Moschitti, A.: Efficient convolution kernels for dependency and constituent syntactic trees. In: Fürnkranz, J., Scheffer, T., Spiliopoulou, M. (eds.) ECML 2006. LNCS (LNAI), vol. 4212, pp. 318–329. Springer, Heidelberg (2006)
15. Severyn, A., Moschitti, A.: Large-scale support vector learning with structural kernels. In: Balcázar, J.L., Bonchi, F., Gionis, A., Sebag, M. (eds.) ECML PKDD 2010, Part III. LNCS (LNAI), vol. 6323, pp. 229–244. Springer, Heidelberg (2010)
16. Sharir, M., Pnueli, A.: Two approaches to interprocedural data flow analysis. In: Program Flow Analysis: Theory and Applications, pp. 189–233. Prentice Hall (1981)
17. Surribas, N.: Wapiti, web application vulnerability scanner/security auditor (2006-2010), http://www.ict-romulus.eu/web/wapiti
18. Tappenden, A., Beatty, P., Miller, J., Geras, A., Smith, M.: Agile security testing of web-based systems via httpunit. In: Proceedings of the Agile Conference, pp. 29–38 (July 2005)
19. Vishwanathan, S., Smola, A.: Fast kernels on strings and trees. In: Proceedings of Neural Information Processing Systems (2002)
20. Wassermann, G., Su, Z.: Static detection of cross-site scripting vulnerabilities. In: ICSE 2008: Proceedings of the 30th International Conference on Software Engineering, pp. 171–180. ACM, New York (2008)
21. Zhang, D., Lee, W.S.: Question classification using support vector machines. In: Proceedings of the 26th Annual International ACM SIGIR Conference on Research and Development in Informaion Retrieval, SIGIR 2003, pp. 26–32. ACM, New York (2003), http://doi.acm.org/10.1145/860435.860443

Robust Requirements Analysis in Complex Systems through Machine Learning

Francesco Garzoli[1], Danilo Croce[1], Manuela Nardini[2],
Francesco Ciambra[2], and Roberto Basili[1]

[1] University of Roma, Tor Vergata, Italy
[2] Finmeccanica SELEX Sistemi Integrati, Italy

Abstract. Requirement Analysis (RA) is a relevant application for Semantic Technologies focused on the extraction and exploitation of knowledge derived from technical documents. Language processing technologies are useful for the automatic extraction of concepts as well as norms (e.g. constraints on the use of devices) that play a key role in knowledge acquisition and design processes. A distributional method to train a kernel-based learning algorithm is here proposed, as a cost-effective approach for the validation stage in RA of Complex Systems, i.e. Naval Combat Systems. The targeted application of Requirement Identification and Information Extraction techniques is here discussed in the realm of robust search processes that allows to suitably locate software functionalities within large collections of requirements written in natural language.

1 Introduction

The objectives of Requirements Engineering (RE) include at least the identification of the goals to be achieved by a target system, the operationalization of such goals into services and constraints, and the assignment of responsibilities for the resulting requirements to agents such as humans, devices and software. Different processes are involved in RE, such as domain analysis, elicitation, specification, assessment, negotiation, documentation and evolution. Sources of information are mostly expressed in natural language and require manual analysis: getting high quality requirements is difficult, critical and costly. During a novel system design, all of these phases must be performed, and generally they are carried out without any reuse of old analysis performed over previous systems.

In this scenario, search systems are usually required to help analysts to locate and access the information stored in documents whereas key-word based search may not be sufficient. As an example, when searching for "*attack scenario*" documents containing an expression such as (the verb) "*assail*" may not be found as for the mismatch between the query and the text. A more semantic aware process is needed to increase the benefits of automatic search in RE. Furthermore the validation of design choices could be automatized, e.g. checking the consistency of requirement pre-conditions. However, translating user requirements and problem domain described in natural language into the consistent modeling of the target application is still challenging. According to [1], "*We are not really*

A. Moschitti and B. Plank (Eds.): EternalS 2013, CCIS 379, pp. 44–58, 2013.

having a problem coding a solution - we are having a problem understanding what solution to code ... If you focus on requirements and verification and validation, the coding will take care of itself". Vagueness and ambiguity are the main phenomena that make the natural language used to describe user requirement a challenging task. Consider the complexity of a sentence when it contains clauses and phrases that describe and relate several objects, conditions, events and/or actions.

Natural Language Processing (NLP) approaches gained much interest in the community of Software Engineering, as recent works in this direction suggest. In [2] a similarity measure based on linguistic information is used for clustering correlated software artifacts. In particular, authors explore the effects of mining lexical information about different artifact element, such as Function Names, Parameter Names or Software Comments. In [3], an automatic approach to classify affordances of web services according to the texts describing them is presented.

Regarding Requirement Analysis, Abbot [4] proposes a technique attempting to guide the systematic procedure that compiles design models from textual requirements. While it was able to produce static analysis and design modules, it was nonetheless requiring high levels of user involvement for decision making. Saeki et. Al. [5] illustrates a process of incrementally constructing software modules from object-oriented specifications as obtained by interpreting text requirements. Nouns were considered as classes and their corresponding verbs as methods. These were automatically extracted from the raw textual descriptions but lexical ambiguity problems and hand-coding were striking limitations in the construction of fully reusable formal specifications. In the REVERE [6] system, a summary of requirements from a natural language text is derived. The system makes use of a lexicon to recognize suitable word senses in the texts. However, no attempt to model the system at the functional level is carried out. In [7] natural language analysis is suggested as a possible approach for automatically compile formalized control mechanisms in the requirement specifications. An expressive semantics-based point cuts within a requirement are detected and mapped into the RDL semi-formal description language. The authors suggest that syntactic and semantic analysis of natural language expressions can be made precise enough to support the definition of a flexible composition mechanism for requirements analysis. All those systems, while exploring the applicability of NLP, propose traditional tools for the specific RE context. Most of the traditional limitations of NLP are thus inherited by the above works, namely costly design and development processes, complex maintenance of the large Knowledge Bases necessary for full NL analysis as well as poor portability across domain, systems and scenarios.

In this work we propose statistical learning methods embedded in a large scale natural language processing system in support of RE. The adoption of advanced technique of NLP combined with Machine Learning capabilities, i.e. Statistical Information Extraction, is a crucial advance to improve applicability of this technology on a large scale. Moreover, the effectiveness of acquired information is evaluated in a Information Retrieval scenario, where a robust search engine has been defined to search existing software functionalities in a specific domain through user requirements expressed in natural language.

In the rest of the paper, Section 2 discusses the application of Human Language Technologies in RE. Section 3 proposes the architecture of an automatic system for Requirement Analysis. Section 4 presents the evaluation of the adopted techniques for the Naval Combat Systems requirement analysis.

2   Language Technologies for Requirement Analysis

The robustness recently achieved by NLP technologies makes their applicability in the support the analysis and design of system development very promising. As an example, the reuse of existing technological components during the design stages of new complex systems can be drastically increased whenever a semantic search system from the targeted component repository is available. Such an engine would be able to rely on conceptual notions in the user queries (e.g. functions and norms), as they are originally extracted from technical specification documents, and retrieve components suitable for the design needs and validate them according to their compliancy or *composability*. The role of Human Language Technologies (HLT) in this proactive support to the analyst is clear as it favors the incremental design through reuse. HLT are crucial to support robust and accurate analysis of unstructured texts, and enrich them by semantic meta-data or other kinds of information implicit in the texts. HLT allows extracting the interesting semantic phenomena and mapping them into structured representation of a target domain. When a semantic meta-model is available, for example in form of an existing ontology, HLT allows to locate concepts in the text (irrespectively from the variable forms in which they appear in the free text), mark them according to Knowledge Representation Languages (such as RDF or OWL) thus unifying different shallow representations of the same concepts. In this way semantic annotations of concepts in the text (i.e. automatic semantic indexes) are obtained for the original document, making it more suitable for clustering, retrieval and browsing activities. In synthesis, HLT enables to perform and simplify several advanced functionalities (e.g. semantic and not keyword based search) that are possible over the text. The semantic annotation task, just outlined above, has been largely studied by the NLP community and it is known as Information Extraction (IE), i.e. *"The identification and extraction of instances of a particular class of events or relationships in a natural language text and their transformation into a structured representation (e.g. a database)."* [8]. IE requires typically three stages. In the first, the target information is abstracted and structured set of inter-related categories are designed. These structures are called *templates* and the categories (roles) that need to be filled with information are called *slots*. For example, if we want to extract conceptual information about vessels from specifications, we may be interested in the name but also in the *type of ship* or its *maximum speed*, as well as its *combat system equipment*. Therefore, a SHIP template can be defined as a conjunctive combination of slots such as *name*, *ship type*, *maximum speed* or *combat system equipment.* Once the template is given, the text fragments containing relevant information to fill the template slots (i.e. specific values associated to the attributes of a certain SHIP instance) need to be identified in a text. The recognition of textual information of interest results from pattern matching against extraction rules. Finally, in a third phase, whenever the information of interest is identified in the text, its mapping in the suitable (e.g. SHIP) template slot is carried out. The above chain is not trivial and contemporary IE systems[1] are usually integrated with large scale knowledge bases, determining all the lexical, syntactic and semantic constraints needed for a correct interpretation of usually domain-specific texts. Unfortunately, the manual development of these resources is a time-consuming task that is often highly error-prone due to the subjectivity and intrinsic vagueness that affects the semantic modeling process. Knowledge acquisition task is often approached through the use of Machine Learning algorithms to automatically learn the domain-specific information from annotated data [9]. Statistical learning methods [10] assume that lexical or grammatical aspects of training data are the basic features for modeling the different inferences. They are then generalized into predictive patterns composing the final induced model. A statistical language processor is assumed to be able to locate specific instances of a template type (e.g. SHIP) and their slot information in an incoming text. The resulting instantiated template can be employed to populate an existing knowledge base whose semantic schema correspond (or can be mapped) to the template structure. Moreover, reasoning over the extracted information, e.g. identifying relations or dependencies with respect to previous requirements, can be better performed. For example, retrieval of developed components that respond properly to new requirements could be realized as a form of reasoning.

3 Machine Learning for Requirement Analysis

In Requirement Analysis some NLP applications like Information Extraction tasks could be very useful to support people to perform this task practically and in a cost-effective way. Statistical NLP approaches provide domain specific models of target interpretation tasks by acquiring and generalizing linguistic observations. Several Statistical Machine Learning paradigms have been defined to provide robust models that easily adapt across different (and possibly specific) domains. These techniques are the basis to our proposed approach and we will discuss them hereafter. This problem is normally treated as a Statistical Classification problem, where the target is to identifying the sub-population to which new data belong, where the identity of the sub-population is unknown (the test data), on the basis of a training set of data containing observations whose sub-population is known (the training data). In this scenario we may be interested for example to induce a template slot for a candidate text. Support Vector Machine (SVM), as discussed in [11] and [12], represents one of the most known learning paradigm for classification, based on Statistical Learning Theory. Given training instances, each one associated with a class and a set of "features", i.e.

---

[1] OpenCalais: http://viewer.opencalais.com/

the dimensions of the employed geometrical representation of each example, the goal of SVM is to produce a model (based on the training data) which predicts the target values of the test data given only the test data features. In a geometric perspective, SVM classifiers learn a decision boundary between two data classes that maximizes the minimum distance or margin from the training points in each class to the boundary. The notion of distance used in such feature space can be adapted to a specific classification problem to better separate examples. This is explicitly the role of kernel functions [11] aiming to separate the learning task from the representation through a proper although implicit mapping to a newer space more expressive for the target problem.

Formally, the $SVM^{multiclass}$ schema described in [13] is applied[2] to implicitly compare all class and select the most likely one, using the multi-class formulation described in [14]. The algorithm thus acquires a specific function $f_y(x)$ for each class $y \in \mathcal{Y}$, with $|\mathcal{Y}| = k$. Given a feature vectors $x \in \mathcal{X}$ representing a novel requisite, $SVM^{multiclass}$ allows to predict a specific class $y^* \in \mathcal{Y}$ by applying the discriminant function $y^* = \arg\max_{\mathbf{y} \in \mathcal{Y}} f_y(x_i)$, where $f_y(x) = w_y \cdot x$ is a linear classifier associated to each y.

3.1 A General Adaptive Architecture for Advanced RA

In this section we present the architecture of a requirement analysis system. It handles Requisite Documents and automatically extracts the information needed in the generic requirement management phase. In the next session, we will discuss how this system can be employed in a real use case as the underlying requirement management phase of a Combat Management System (CMS) is presented. This system processes semi-structured documents, i.e. written in natural language, and enriches texts with linguistic information employed by other modules. Then, all sentences expressing one or more requisites are retrieved and the target information is extracted. Interesting slots of the *templates* modeling different concepts in the requirement analysis are filled. These template instances are used to populate the *Requirement Repository* that can be later easily accessed by the analyst. Moreover, the system also analyzes the extracted information in order to recognize/acquire existing dependencies among different requisites.

In Figure 1, the overall architecture is shown and the interaction between the different functions that contribute to the main workflow, as well as their interactions and dependencies are reported. On the top of the architecture, the basic Natural Language Processing (NLP) chain is foreseen. This module carries out different NL steps needed to analyze a document, extracting all linguistic information useful to later modules in the chain. This includes steps such as a Sentence Splitter, a Part-of-Speech tagger, a Name Entity recognizer, a Word Sense Disambiguation module and a Syntactic Parser. These modules are based on different knowledge bases, modeling different aspects of the overall RA process:

---

[2] http://svmlight.joachims.org/svm_multiclass.html

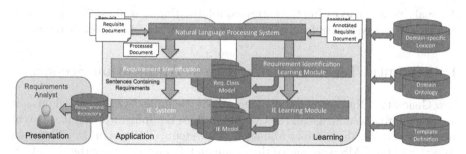

Fig. 1. Requisite Analysis System Architecture

- *Domain specific Lexicon*: it contains the specific domain dictionaries providing lexical information about the application domain, e.g. involved entities and acronyms.
- *Domain ontology*: it provides an ontological model of the application domain, as well as an abstraction of the requirements (i.e. the template for the Information Extraction activity). Moreover it provides the relations among different requirements, e.g. dependency rules among pre-conditions and post-conditions that enable the reasoning.
- *Template Definition*: it represents the repository of different templates involved in the IE activity, that are domain specific (as the ontology), but possibly more specific than the concepts or relations in the domain ontology.

According to our machine learning perspective, each module performs the corresponding task according to a model of the domain that has been automatically previously acquired from real data. These are requirement documents that have been previously annotated by the analysts, with the same information the IE system is expected to precisely detect in future texts. The general architecture is thus divided in different main blocks to distinguish models directly employed in the (on-line, i.e. interactive) Requirement Analysis Application workflow from the ones employed in the (*off-line*) Learning workflow. In the *Application Block* the following modules process requirement as follows:

- *Requirement Identification Module*: This module performs the analysis of documents that are enriched with linguistic information in order to suitably locate sentences containing concepts (and relations) of interest in the requirements analysis domain.
- *Information Extraction (IE) System*: Once a specific requisite is found, the extraction of its relevant information is carried out as a slot-filling process over the existing templates. Once a template is filled, it is made available (i.e. it populates) the Requirement Repository for the analysis.

In a machine learning perspective, each module performs the corresponding task according to a model of the domain that must be automatically acquired from annotated data. In this view, the second block in the architecture of Figure 1, i.e. the *Learning* block, is dedicated to the acquisition of the individual IE models. Finally, the *Presentation* block is responsible for the interaction with the analysts in (1) accessing the extracted information as well as (2) in providing feedback to the system in form of acceptance or rejection of some of its decisions.

4   Semantic Technologies in a Real Application Scenario

New Generation Naval Combat Systems are very complex systems based on a sw component able to manage all the Combat System Equipment (CSE) in different mission scenarios: the Combat Management System (CMS) as in [15]. The main objective of the CMS is to enable the Command Team to manage the ships CSE to conduct the missions in the scenarios. The CMS is mainly composed of a real time component (C2S) which provides the Combat System with facilities for the management of short term activities (Conduct of action); and a Command Support System (CSS), which provides the Combat System with facilities for the management of medium and long term activities in the conduct of operational tasks. From the functional point of view the C2S is decomposed into application segments that allow the system to perform the following functions:

1. global tactical picture compilation,
2. warfare missions conduction in different domains (Air, Surface, Submarine, Land) at platform and force level,
3. Tactical Data Link exchange data functions.

Each functional requirement of CMS is allocated to Computer Software Configuration Items (CSCI). CSCIs communicate exchanging data over the ship network through a common application layer. The communication principles are different according to the relationships among the components that communicate each other. Independently of the communication model the strategy is that each sw component shares data with the other system components to enable them, i.e. allow them to carry out their own functionalities. A key aspect for managing the overall CMS complexity is the design and description of CSCI interactions in terms of data each component has to *publish* for the benefit of the users. A system like the CMS has a large number of users, a large number of connections to CSE and heavy requirement on the processing applications that must be executed in real-time. Further constraints are given by the demanding performances, security requirements and by the incorporation of Off-The-Shelf software. It is clear how this class of systems needs clear requirement description and management throughout its entire system life cycle. The introduction of Semantic Technologies such as IE (as described in previous sections) in the Requirement Analysis process of naval CMS is bringing significant benefits in different phases of project life cycle. In particular, the application of Machine Learning techniques in the initial phase of the project has allowed filling the gap between the contractual technical specifications and system design description. Thanks to the machine learning method, the tool illustrated in this paper automates the process of recognition of several inferences about system components directly from the texts that characterize them, i.e. the requirements.

4.1   Experimental Evaluation

Machine-learning techniques for requirement analysis described in the previous Sections have been implemented in a Requirement Analysis System, according to the Architecture shown in Figure 1. The resulting adaptive system has been applied to a real scenario, i.e. the requirement analysis of a Naval Combat Systems, focusing on the SW system, namely the Combat Management System (CMS). This Section provides the empirical evaluation of system functionalities, such as the *Requirement Identification* (RI) and *Information Extraction* (IE) as applied to the CMS requirement analysis. Requisites here refer to different aspects of the CMS, such as *Functional Requirements* (FNC) or *Performance requirements* (PRF). The dataset adopted in our tests is made of 4,727 annotated requirements, related to three different scenarios, called *EAU, FREMM* and *NUM*. Each requisite has been labeled according to one of the five requisite types, which are specific aspects of the resulting system, such as FNC or PRF, as shown in Table 1.

Table 1. Requisite Types

ABBR	Type	Number
NFC	Non-Functional Requirements	74
DCC	Design and Construction Constraints	288
OPR	Operator requirements	2,587
PRF	Performance Requirements	249
FNC	Functional requirements	1,529
Total		4,727

The *Requirement Identification* system of Figure 1 has been trained to recognize and characterize requirements. The module applies Support Vector Machine classification to associate each requirement its suitable specific class, reflected into the corresponding type. Different models of observable text properties allowed to investigate different linguistic information and to identify the most informative representations for the learning algorithm:

- The *Bag-of-Word* (*BoW*) model mainly accounts for the lexical information: requisites are mapped into sets of words, neglecting word order, i.e. syntactic information.
- The *N-gram of Words* (*N-Words*) model provides a first form of grammatical information, by mapping short word sequences into n-grams of words.
- A *Bag-of-Word* and *N-gram of Part-of-Speech* (*N-POS*) introduces grammatical information as it attaches part-of-speech to n-grams, by further generalizing the sequences of words in the textual requisite.
- The *Comprehensive* (*BoW + N-Words + N-POS*) model accounts for all the previous information, i.e. as it includes Bag-of-Words, n-grams of Words and n-grams of Part-of-Speeches.

The objective of the experiments is also to measure and compare the adaption capabilities of SVM classifiers to different scenarios: the idea is that SVMs should be able to induce meaningful classification models from the data available in a specific scenario, i.e. the *in-domain* scenario, but also provide accurate predictions even when applied to different, i.e. *out-of-domain*, scenarios.

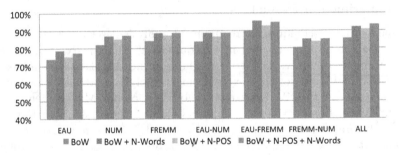

Fig. 2. Requisite Classification Results

Figure 2 reports the classification results, in terms of *accuracy*, i.e. the percentage of correctly classified requisites. Different colors reflect the different adopted feature models. The first three histograms provide results when classifiers are trained over requisite from one single scenario (i.e. EAU, NUM and FREMM respectively) and applied to the other remaining scenarios. The second group of histograms shows results when classifiers are trained over two scenarios (i.e. (EAU-NUM), (EAU-FREMM) and (FREMM-NUM)) and applied to requisites in the single remaining scenario. Finally, the last group shows results from an *in-domain* setting, when the 80% of requisites from all scenarios are used to train classifiers, while the remaining 20% are used as test set. In all experiments, SVM parameters are estimated over an held-out 20% of the training data. Results, especially when lexical and grammatical features are considered, i.e. the *BoW + N-words + N-POS* model, are very good and an accuracy higher of 93% is achieved. Moreover, the system robustness is very promising, as accuracy higher than 85% is reached even in *out-of-domain* tests. Errors refer to reasonable and genuinely ambiguous cases. For example, the system labels as FNC both requisites *"The CMS shall display the progress of each engagement."* and *"The CMS shall display single manoeuvre request within ..."*, although this latter is associated to OPR. Once a specific requisite is located, the *Information Extraction* (IE) System (Fig. 1) carries out the extraction of its relevant information, as a slot-filling process over the reference templates. Templates are automatically generated from the analysis of a *Domain Ontology*, which provided a model of the application domain as well as an abstraction of individual requirement types. These types ontologically determine different *capabilities*, i.e. desired characteristics of a target system. Moreover, the ontology provides hierarchies that group capabilities according to their semantics and the expected grain of analysis. Coarse grained capabilities refer to high level system characteristics, such as such RESOURCE MANAGEMENT, that in turn groups together several fine-grained capabilities. These latter specialize the considered aspects, e.g. NAVIGATION RADAR(NAV), that specializes the notion of *Resource Management in Navigation Radar systems*. The IE system is asked to associate a requisite like *"The CMS shall monitor information transmitted by the Navigation Radar"* to the NAV template, recognizing its finer-grained aspect. The database of *Templates*, defined by the ontology, includes 65 templates that correspond to the range of the function mapping each requisite to its corresponding template. The high number of target class makes this task very challenging with respect to the previous requisite identification problem.

SVM classifiers have been employed even in this task: parameter estimation has not been employed, to prove the low dependence of the learning algorithm from external parameters; instead, results are reported as mean accuracy and (negligible) standard deviation in parenthesis. Requisites are here represented similarly to the previous task, thus employing the *BoW* model, that consider only lexical information, and the *BoW + N-Words* model that consider also the shallow syntactic information of the requisites. In term of percentage of requisite correctly covered by a template we have a classification results 87,61% (1,16%) with **Bow** models and 88,5% (1,46%) with **BoW + N-Words** model. Even in this evaluation, results show an accuracy of 88% proving the IE system as a largely applicable process.

4.2   Retrieval in Large Repositories of Software Documentation

In this section the contribution of the proposed approach for Requirements Analysis (RA) is investigated in an Information Retrieval scenario to improve the software reusability. In order to retrieve a piece of software or any other existing functionality that satisfies a specific user requirement, a Requirement Analyst usually retrieves existing documentation through a search engine through specific term-based queries. In a Ad-hoc Retrieval scenario [12], the quality of the retrieved material is strictly dependent from the expressed query that reflects user needs. In this section we instead define a robust search engine to enable the Requirement Analyst the retrieval of existing software functionalities by expressing software requirements in natural language.

The contribution of the proposed architecture is shown here to enable a more conceptual kind of search. The idea is that requirements determine complex queries can be processed by our RA software and used to retrieve existing software *compatible* with the functionalities expressed by the user requirements. More formally, the user express a requisite $r_i \in R$ in order to retrieve one of the specific functionalities $f_1^i, \ldots, f_{n_i}^i$ satisfying r_i. We denote the set of all $\{f_j^i | j = 1, \ldots, n_i\}$ as F_i and $n_i = |F_i|$. As an example, given a requisite r "*The CS shall provide facilities for Human Computer Interface presentation*", we would like to retrieve the implemented functionalities satisfying the specific need, such as the functionality f "*The CMS shall provide the following facilities at CMS consoles : screens, pointing device, keyboards, MFKA, service settings.*". In fact, in this case, the requisite r is satisfied by f, because it expresses the available facilities to interact with the software system. We collected all the pairs $RF = \{\langle r_i, F_i \rangle\}$, where r_i is a system requirement and F_i is the set of the corresponding functionalities satisfying r_i, denoted by $\{f_1^i, f_2^i, \ldots, f_{n_i}^i\}$.

To associate a generic f to a given r, we first exploit the vector representation described in Section 4.1 that reflects the generic notion of semantic text similarity [16,17]. This is a geometric representation of textual meaning based on the the set of lexical and grammatical features expressed in the resulting weighted vector that establishes a variety of latent semantic relations between requirements: the closer two requirements are in the representation space, the stronger is their semantic relation.

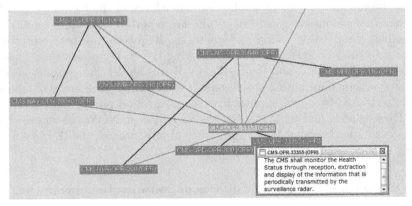

Fig. 3. Conceptual Graph employed to evaluate the semantic similarity function

A first use of this representation is the Graphical User Interface (GUI) to the database, that allows to analyze complex semantic relationships between individual requisites, such as the redundancy. As shown in Figure 3, individual requisites are represented through a conceptual graph where edges between vertices express weighted semantic similarity relationship between two instances. In Figure 3 the graph of requisites closer to the requisite **CMS-OPR-3333**, i.e. "*The CMS shall monitor the equipment Status through reception, extraction and display of the information that is periodically transmitted by the surveillance radar ...*" is shown. Notice how the most similar text is **CMS-OPR-33355**: "*The CMS shall monitor the Health Status through reception, extraction and display of the information that is periodically transmitted by the surveillance radar.*". This confirms that the captured notion of similarity well reflects rich semantic relations. This relationship instance is in fact a form of *textual entailment* [18], i.e. the directional relationship between a text pair $\langle T, H \rangle$, made by T, i.e. the entailing "*Text*", and H, i.e. the entailed "*Hypothesis*". It is usually stated that T entails H if a human that reads T (assuming it to be true) would accept that H is most likely true. This definition is somewhat informal but model an underlying useful form of commonsense knowledge for human expert.

The way a graph is built depends on the distance metrics established within the underlying vector space. Given a requisite r_i, the short texts describing functionalities f_j can be ranked according to their semantic similarity with the specific r_i, modeled through the cosine similarity sim between the corresponding vectors $\overrightarrow{r_i}$ and $\overrightarrow{f_j}$: $sim(r_i, f_j) = \frac{\overrightarrow{r_i} \cdot \overrightarrow{f_j}}{||\overrightarrow{r_i}|| \cdot ||\overrightarrow{f_j}||}$

In this evaluation, we considered a set of 290 requisites and 1,474 functionalities of the Combat Management System (CMS). The mean number of functionalities for each r was 5, with a standard deviation of about 3.5. For each r_i, the set F_i specifies all functionalities realizing r_i: these are the gold standard, i.e. the set of texts expected to be retrieved by the analyst querying by r_i. As they are short texts, individual r_i as well as f_j are modeled according to the *Comprehensive* model, i.e. the *BoW + N-POS + N-Words* vector representation, as it achieves the best results in the RA discussed in Section 4.1.

The information acquired during the RA phase is here exploited in order to define a *Re-ranking* phase: the ranking provided by the semantic similarity function is thus adjusted to filter out all those functionalities that do not share the same characterization of the target requirement r_i, i.e. the same *type* and *capability*, as discussed in Section 4.1. Four different retrieval strategies are applied, giving rise to four IR systems:

- **NoFilter**: for each r_i, the most similar f_j are retrieved and ranked according to *sim*: no filter is applied.
- **Type**: the ranking provided by *sim* is grouped in two lists: the first, ranked higher, is made by functionalities sharing the same type of r_i and a second list including the remaining f_j whose type is different. In this way functionalities f_j of the same type of r_i are always ranked first than the other ones.
- **Capability**: the two lists are created as before with respect to the capability assigned to the target r_i, so that functionalities with the same capabilities of r_i are ranked first;
- **Type+Capability**: the ranking provided by *sim* is modified as before according to the sharing the both type *and* capability of r_i.

Different strategies are evaluated according to standard IR evaluation metrics: *Precision (P)*, *Recall (R)*, *F-measure (F1)* and *Mean Average Precision (MAP)*. Precision is expressed as $P = \frac{tp}{tp+fp}$, where tp is the number of the relevant functionalities retrieved, and fp is the number of the not relevant functionalities retrieved. Recall is expressed as $R = \frac{tp}{tp+fn}$, where fn is the number of the relevant functionalities not retrieved. While Precision estimates the capacity to retrieve correct functionalities, Recall is more interesting in this scenario as it measures system capacity to retrieve all existing functionalities; in many cases, it is more important to retrieve all existing software instead of spending more time reading useless documentation. F-measure consider both aspects as it is estimated as the harmonic mean of Precision and Recall: $F1 = \frac{2 \cdot P \cdot R}{P+R}$

Finally, MAP provides a single accuracy measure across different recall levels. MAP is based on the oracle given by $RF = \{\langle r_i, F_i \rangle\}$ that are pairs of a requisite r_i and a functionality set F_i. Every requisite r_i also corresponds to a ranked list of retrieved functionalities, ordered according to the similarity function *sim*. Let F_i^k be the list of retrieved functionalities f_j^i from the top result (i.e. f_1^i, ranked as the closest by the system) to the f_k^i that corresponds to the position where k-th members of the functionalities in F_i results all returned. In this way, the

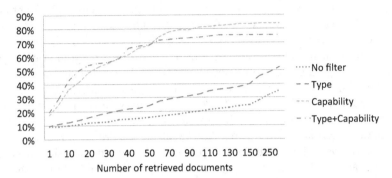

Fig. 4. System Recall

number of true positive functionalities for a requirement is exactly k. Then, the *Mean Average Precision* at level k of recall is denoted as:

$$MAP@k = \frac{1}{|RF|} \sum_{i=1}^{|RF|} \frac{1}{|F_i^k|} \sum_{k=1}^{|F_i^k|} P(F_i^k)$$

where $|F_i^k|$ obviously denotes the number of relevant functionalities for a given requisite r_i that varies with i, and $P(F_i^k)$ expresses the precision against the first k true positives for r_i. The results in terms of Recall with respect to increasing number of retrieved functionalities are shown in Figure 4 for different retrieval strategies. Moreover, Table 2 report evaluation figures for varying size of the retrieved document lists.

Table 2. Accuracy for different IR strategies and sizes of returned functionalities

		1	5	10	15	20	25	30	35	40	45	50
No filter	P	0,158	0,036	0,021	0,016	0,014	0,012	0,011	0,010	0,010	0,009	0,008
	R	0,092	0,093	0,102	0,107	0,122	0,124	0,128	0,142	0,147	0,152	0,160
	F1	0,116	0,052	0,035	0,028	0,026	0,022	0,020	0,019	0,018	0,017	0,016
Type	P	0,175	0,046	0,029	0,024	0,022	0,020	0,018	0,017	0,016	0,015	0,015
	R	0,097	0,112	0,126	0,141	0,157	0,178	0,196	0,211	0,219	0,226	0,242
	F1	0,125	0,065	0,047	0,042	0,038	0,036	0,033	0,032	0,030	0,029	0,028
Capability	P	0,407	0,151	0,106	0,085	0,073	0,065	0,060	0,056	0,052	0,051	0,049
	R	0,176	0,255	0,363	0,415	0,484	0,525	0,553	0,588	0,615	0,659	0,680
	F1	0,246	0,189	0,165	0,141	0,127	0,116	0,108	0,102	0,097	0,094	0,091
Type+Capability	P	0,488	0,167	0,113	0,089	0,073	0,066	0,060	0,055	0,050	0,047	0,044
	R	0,196	0,296	0,430	0,497	0,538	0,553	0,561	0,585	0,661	0,677	0,683
	F1	0,280	0,214	0,179	0,150	0,128	0,118	0,109	0,101	0,093	0,088	0,083

Moreover, in Table 3 the results of MAP are reported: rows correspond to different strategies while columns report different MAP values obtained when k is fixed to 1, 2 and 5, respectively. When no filter is applied, results are quite low, especially in term of Recall: when 50 functionalities are retrieved only 20% are usually relevant for the user. The high-level filter, represented by the *Type* strategy, improves results even if the difference is not very relevant. The Capability information produces a considerable improvement: when 50 functionalities are retrieved, more than 70% of them are relevant for the user. The filter that considers both type and capability is quite effective when few items are retrieved, as confirmed by the highest value of MAP achieved for lower levels of k.

Table 3. Mean Average Precision

Filter	MAP@1	MAP@2	MAP@5
No filter	0.139	0.126	0.117
Type	0.149	0.142	0.135
Capability	0.305	0.284	0.273
Type+Capability	0.368	0.354	0.347

Finally, a qualitative analysis of the retrieval accuracy can be carried out by studying some examples of returned functionalities. We queried the IR service by a system requirement r such as *"The CS shall provide facilities for Human Computer Interface presentation"*. Table 4 shows the retrieved functionalities obtained by applying the combined filter (*type* and *capability*) to the input r. It is clear that the returned functionalities have a quite good relevance for the queries requisite, as the first hits in the Table show. Moreover, the quality of the relevance decrease along with the ranking: the third returned hit is much less relevant than the first two, despite properly respond to the requirement.

Table 4. Example of retrieved functionalities

r	*The CS shall provide facilities for Human Computer Interface presentation*
f_1^r	*The CMS shall provide similar controls and means of interaction with all displays, i.e. they should be the same where possible and consistent otherwise.*
f_2^r	*The CMS shall provide the following facilities at CMS consoles : screens, pointing device, keyboards, MFKA, service settings.*
f_3^r	*The CMS shall display alerts on primary view area*

5   Conclusions

While Semantic Technologies show a large set of promises in the Defense System Engineering domain, they are usually very demanding from the point of view of complexity in design, optimization and maintenance. Traditional (i.e. Knowledge-based) HLTs approaches are in this class of technologies. The results achieved in Statistical Natural Language Processing by the adoption of robust and accurate Machine Learning algorithms allowed to increase the applicability of these methods in several domain, from Business Analysis, Web Communication as well Security. In this paper, a general architecture for large scale and adaptive Requirement Analysis has been presented. Its application to Requirement Analysis in the specific Defense System Engineering domain is evaluated and discussed. The main idea is to combine requirement classification and IE for automation of most of the validation stages related to system behaviors. The system is currently experimented in a specific scenario of Combat System Equipment, applied to the management of the design and description of the Computer Software Configuration Items interactions. The application of semantic technologies in the Defense System Engineering domain has shown its potentials in the

Requirement Analysis process. In particular it can support significant cost reduction, products' quality enhancement as well as the improvement of Engineering processes.

References

1. Cook, D.: Evolution of programming languages and why a language is not enough to solve our problems (1999), http://lsc.fie.umich.mx/juan/Materias/FIE/Lenguajes/Slides/Papers/Evolution.html
2. Corazza, A., Di Martino, S., Maggio, V., Scanniello, G.: Combining machine learning and information retrieval techniques for software clustering. In: Moschitti, A., Scandariato, R. (eds.) EternalS 2011. CCIS, vol. 255, pp. 42–60. Springer, Heidelberg (2012)
3. Bennaceur, A., Johansson, R., Moschitti, A., Spalazzese, R., Sykes, D., Saadi, R., Issarny, V.: Inferring affordances using learning techniques. In: Moschitti, A., Scandariato, R. (eds.) EternalS 2011. CCIS, vol. 255, pp. 79–87. Springer, Heidelberg (2012)
4. Abbott, R.J.: Program design by informal English descriptions. Communications of the ACM 26(11), 882–894 (1983)
5. Saeki, M., Horai, H., Enomoto, H.: Software development process from natural language specification. In: Proceedings of the 11th International Conference on Software Engineering, New York, NY, USA, pp. 64–73 (1989)
6. Sawyer, P., Rayson, P., Garside, R.: Revere: Support for requirements synthesis from documents. Information Systems Frontiers 4(3), 343–353 (2002)
7. Chitchyan, R., Rashid, A., Rayson, P., Waters, R.: Semantics-based composition for aspect-oriented requirements engineering. In: Proceedings of AOSD, pp. 36–48. ACM, New York (2007)
8. Grishman, R.: Information extraction: Techniques and challenges. In: Pazienza, M.T. (ed.) SCIE 1997. LNCS, vol. 1299, pp. 10–27. Springer, Heidelberg (1997)
9. Manning, C.D., Schütze, H.: Foundations of statistical natural language processing. MIT Press, Cambridge (1999)
10. Gildea, D., Jurafsky, D.: Automatic Labeling of Semantic Roles. Computational Linguistics 28(3), 245–288 (2002)
11. Vapnik, V.N.: The Nature of Statistical Learning Theory. Springer, New York (1995)
12. Basili, R., Moschitti, A.: Automatic Text Categorization: from Information Retrieval to Support Vector Learning. Aracne (2005)
13. Joachims, T., Finley, T., Yu, C.N.: Cutting-plane training of structural SVMs. Machine Learning 77(1), 27–59 (2009)
14. Crammer, K., Singer, Y.: On the algorithmic implementation of multi-class SVMS. Journal of Machine Learning Research 2, 265–292 (2001)
15. Ciambra, F., Nardini, M.: Naval combat system design: System engineering approach and complexity management. In: Proceedings of INCOSE, France (2004)
16. Agirre, E., Cer, D., Diab, M., Gonzalez-Agirre, A.: Semeval-2012 task 6: A pilot on semantic textual similarity. In: *SEM 2012: The First Joint Conference on Lexical and Computational Semantics, Montréal, Canada (2012)
17. Mihalcea, R., Corley, C., Strapparava, C.: Corpus-based and knowledge-based measures of text semantic similarity. In: AAAI 2006 (2006)
18. Dagan, I., Glickman, O.: Probabilistic Textual Entailment: Generic Applied Modeling of Language Variability. In: Learning Methods for Text Understanding and Mining (January 2004)

Automatic Generation and Reranking
of SQL-Derived Answers to NL Questions

Alessandra Giordani and Alessandro Moschitti

Department of Computer Science and Engineering,
University of Trento, Italy

Abstract. In this paper, given a relational database, we automatically translate a natural language question into an SQL query retrieving the correct answer. We exploit the structure of the DB to generate a set of candidate SQL queries, which we rerank with a SVM-ranker based on tree kernels. In particular we use linguistic dependencies in the natural language question and the DB metadata to build a set of plausible SELECT, WHERE and FROM clauses enriched with meaningful joins. Then, we combine all the clauses to get the set of all possible SQL queries, producing candidate queries to answer the question. This approach can be recursively applied to deal with complex questions, requiring nested queries. We sort the candidates in terms of scores of correctness using a weighting scheme applied to the query generation rules. Then, we use a SVM ranker trained with structural kernels to reorder the list of question and query pairs, where both members are represented as syntactic trees. The f-measure of our model on standard benchmarks is in line with the best models (85% on the first question), which use external and expensive hand-crafted resources such as the semantic interpretation. Moreover, we can provide a set of candidate answers with a Recall of the answer of about 92% and 96% on the first 2 and 5 candidates, respectively.

1 Introduction

In the last decade, a variety of approaches have been developed to automatically convert natural language questions into machine-readable instructions. In the area of databases, question answering systems are supposed to answer a natural language question by executing a SQL query. This is obviously a complex task as systems have to deal with the lexical gap between natural language expressions and database structure. In this paper, we will demonstrate that it is possible to fill such gap by relying on (i) the informative metadata embedded in all real databases, (ii) natural language processing methods, e.g., syntactic parsing, and (iii) advanced machine learning to build kernel-based rerankers.

When designing a database, domain experts are requested to organize entities and relationships naming tables and columns in a meaningful way (i.e. *state_name* or *capital* instead of *table_1* or *table_2*). Moreover the database schema also specifies constraints and data types. This metadata is stored in an underlying database that contains tables of each database. The latter, in turn,

A. Moschitti and B. Plank (Eds.): EternalS 2013, CCIS 379, pp. 59–76, 2013.

contain columns referring to table names and column names. Such logic organization is referred to as *catalog*, and in SQL systems it is stored in a database
called INFORMATION_SCHEMA (IS for brevity). A fragment sample is shown in
Figure 1. IS can be inspected as a normal database, posing SQL queries to obtain
useful fields to build a new SQL query.

Instead of using tailored dictionaries, we can enrich our knowledge based on
the metadata added by the domain expert, when designing the database. For
example, an answer for the question *"Which rivers run through New York"* can
be found in the GeoQuery corpus (whose structure is stored in IS as shown in
Figure 1).

While we have a simple matching for the word *rivers* with table *river* and
column *river_name*, there isn't a direct mapping between the word *run* in the
question and any of the columns in the metadata. However, the disambiguation of
the term *run* can be easily performed by looking at the less semantically distant
metadata entry, i.e., *traverse*. This matching is re-confirmed when investigating
on all possible interpretations of *New York* in this database (i.e. city_name,
state_name, etc.), by the existing reference between column *traverse* in table
river and column *state_name* in table state.

However, a link between both words *New* and *York* is not so easy, since there
is no evidence of relatedness between the two words in the metadata: this means
that the whole database should be looked up for their stems. Words can be
matched with lots of values (e.g., "New York" both as city and as state name,
but also with "New Jersey"), as shown by Figure 2. We can generate all possible
(even ambiguous) queries exploiting related metadata information (i.e. primary
and foreign keys, constraints, datatypes, etc.) and select the most plausible one
using a re-ranker.

Last but no least, we deal with complex natural language (NL) questions,
containing subordinates, conjunctions and negations and nested SQL queries. In
particular, we designed a mapping algorithm that matches dependencies between
NL components and SQL structure that allows to build a set of possible queries
that answers a given question.

TABLES

TABLE_SCHEMA	TABLE_NAME	...
geoquery	state	
geoquery	city	
geoquery	river	
geoquery	border	
geoquery	highlow	
...	...	

COLUMNS

TABLE_SCHEMA	TABLE_NAME	COLUMN_NAME	DATA_TYPE	...
geoquery	state	state_name	varchar	
geoquery	state	population	float	
geoquery	city	city_name	varchar	
geoquery	city	state_name	varchar	
geoquery	river	traverse	varchar	
...			...	

KEY_COL_USAGE

TABLE_SCHEMA	TABLE_NAME	COLUMN_NAME	REFERENCED_TABLE_SCHEMA	REFERENCED_TABLE_NAME	REFERENCED_COLUMN_NAME	...
geoquery	city	state_name	geoquery	state	state_name	
geoquery	river	traverse	geoquery	state	state_name	
...						

Fig. 1. A DBMS catalog containing GEOQUERY and SAKILA

CITY_NAME	STATE_NAME	POPULATION	...
new york	new york	7071640	
newark	new jersey	329248	
...			

STATE_NAME	CAPITAL	POPULATION	...
new york	albany	17558000	
new jersey	trenton	7365000	
...			

RIVER_NAME	TRAVERSE	...
delaware	new york	
delaware	new jersey	
allegheny	new york	
hudson	new york	
hudson	new jersey	
...		

Fig. 2. GeoQuery database fragment

Section 2 gives a formal description of the problem while Section 3 describes the basic steps of our algorithm used to build clause. Section 4 shows how we prune and weigh queries in their possible combinations to generate an ordered set of meaningful queries among which we find the answer. Section 5 describes tree kernels our kernel-based rerankers. Section 6 discusses the results obtained using a reranking algorithm, while Section 7 draws some conclusions.

2   The Problem

We will begin by introducing the notion of typed dependencies and how to obtain a collapsed list of dependencies starting from an NL sentence. Then we will introduce the subset of Structured Query Language that our system can deal with and, in order to formalize the problem, we will recall the notation of corresponding operations in relational algebra.

2.1   NL Questions and Dependencies List

To represent the textual relationships of the NL sentence we use typed dependency relations. The Stanford Dependencies representation [8] provides a simple and consistent description of the binary grammar relations existing between a governor and a dependent. As shown in the example below, each dependency is written as *abbreviated_relation_name* (governor, dependent). The governor and the dependent are words in the sentence associated with a number indicating the position of the word in the sentence.

In particular we refer to collapsed representation, where dependencies involving prepositions, conjuncts, as well as information about the referent of relative clauses are collapsed to get direct dependencies between content words.

For example, the Stanford Dependencies Collapsed (SDC) representation for the question, q_1: *"What are the capitals of the states that border the most populated state?"* is the following:

$SDC_{q_1} = attr$(are-2, what-1), $root$(ROOT-0, are-2),
det(capitals-4, the-3), $nsubj$(are-2, capitals-4),
$nsubj$(border-9, states-7), $rcmod$(states-7, border-9),
det(states-13, the-10), $advmod$(populated-12, most-11),
$amod$(state-13, populated-12), $dobj$(borders-9, state-13)

The current representation contains approximately 53 grammatical relations but for our purposes we only use the following: adverbial and adjectival modifier, agent, complement, object, subject, relative clause modifier, prepositional modifier, and root.

2.2 SQL Queries and Relational Algebra

The general SQL query with which our system can deal has the following form:

$$\text{SELECT } COLUMN \text{ FROM } TABLE \text{ [WHERE } CONDITION] \tag{1}$$

The query is interpreted starting from the relation in the FROM clause, selecting tuples that satisfy the condition indicated in the WHERE clause (optional) and then projecting the attribute in the SELECT clause.

In relational algebra, selection and projection are performed by σ and π operators respectively. The meaning of the SQL query above is the same as that of the relational expression:

$$\pi_{COLUMN}\left(\sigma_{CONDITION}(TABLE)\right) \tag{2}$$

It is worth noting that while relational algebra formally applies to sets of tuples (i.e. relations), in a DBMS relations are bags so it may contain duplicate tuples [3]. For our purposes the fact of having duplicates in the result adds nois; this is why we always delete multiple copies of a tuple by using the keyword DISTINCT in the $COLUMN$ field. In our QA task we expect that questions can be answered with a single result set (e.g. we can deal with *"Cities in Texas"* and *"Populations in Texas"* but not with the combined query *"Cities and their population in Texas"*). That is, even if in general $COLUMN$ could be a - possibly empty - list of attributes, in our system it just contains one attribute. We can apply to this attribute aggregation operators that summarize it by means of SUM, AVG, MIN, MAX and COUNT, always combined with DISTINCT keyword (e.g. SELECT COUNT(DISTINCT state.state_name)).

Instead, $CONDITION$ is a logical expression where basic conditions, in the form e_L OP e_R, with OP=$\{<,>,$LIKE,IN$\}$, are combined with AND, OR, NOT operators. While e_L is always in the form table.column, e_R could be:

– numerical value (e.g. city.population > 15000) or
– string value (e.g. city.state_name LIKE "Texas") or
– nested query (e.g. city.city_name IN (SELECT state. capital FROM state)

An example of a complex WHERE condition could be the following:
city.population > 15000 AND city.city_name NOT IN (SELECT state.capital FROM state)) AND NOT city.state_name LIKE "Texas" (i.e. *"major non-capital cities excluding texas"*).

The meaning of $TABLE$ is more straightforward, since it should contain table name(s) to which the other two clauses refer. This clause could just be a single relation or a join operation, which selectively pairs tuples of two relations. We only deal with theta-joins where we take the Cartesian product of two relations and exclusively select those tuples that satisfy a condition C. The notation for theta-joins of relations R and S based on condition C is $R{\bowtie}S \atop C$. We use the SQL keyword ON to keep this condition C separated from the other WHERE conditions since it reflects a database requirement and shouldn't match to anything of the NL question. (e.g. `city JOIN state ON city.city_name = state.capital`).

The complexity of generated queries is fairly high indeed, since we can deal with questions that require nesting, aggregation and negation in addition to basic projection, selection and joining (e.g. *"How many states have major non-capital cities excluding Texas"*).

2.3 Problem Definition

The question answering task of finding an SQL query that retrieves an answer for a given NL question reduces to the following problem.

Given a question q represented by means of one typed dependency collapsed list SDC_q, generate the three sets of clauses $\mathcal{S}, \mathcal{F}, \mathcal{W}$ (argument of SELECT, FROM and WHERE, respectively) such that:

$$\exists s \in \mathcal{S}, \exists f \in \mathcal{F}, \exists w \in \mathcal{W} \text{ s.t. } \pi_s \left(\sigma_w(f) \right) \text{ answers q} \tag{3}$$

The query *answer* $\pi_s \left(\sigma_w(f) \right)$ is chosen among the set of all possible queries $\mathcal{A} = \{\text{SELECT } s \times \text{ FROM } f \times \text{ WHERE } w\}$ in a way that maximizes the probability of generating a result set answering question q.

3 Building Clauses Sets

In order to generate all possible queries for a question q we need to find their possible SELECT, FROM and WHERE clauses ($\mathcal{S}, \mathcal{F}$ and $\mathcal{W}$). We start from a dependency list SDC_q and (a) prune and stem its components, (b) add synonyms, (c) create the set of stems used to build $\mathcal{S}$ and $\mathcal{W}$ and (d) keep only dependencies possibly used in the recursive step to generate nested queries. Building the set $\mathcal{F}$ from $\mathcal{S}$ and $\mathcal{W}$ is straightforward.

We are now going to briefly discuss some examples to introduce the objective of individual steps and clarify how the entire process is carried out. The first question we take into account is the simplest one: *"What is the capital of Texas?"*. Its answer can be retrieved executing the query: `SELECT capital FROM state WHERE state.state_name='Texas'`. We can see that they share only two stems, *capital* and *Texas*. The key of categorizing stems (Section 3.2) is to recognize that the first stem will be used in $\mathcal{S}$ and the second one in $\mathcal{W}$. In particular, since the word *Texas* is not a value in the *IS*, it is used as a r-value in the WHERE expression, while the l-value is derived from the column name under where it appears (Section 3.4).

The fact of being respectively projection and selection oriented can be inferred looking at their grammar relations, i.e. inspecting the dependency list (e.g. root of the sentence together subject dependent are typically used for projections). This list needs to be preprocessed (section 3.1) to take into account only relevant relations between the *stems* of the question. Let us consider for example the question: *"What is the capital of the most populous state?"* and its associated answering query SELECT capital FROM state WHERE population = (SELECT max(population) FROM state).

The matching words are *capital* and *state*, while stemming also allows to find a mapping through *popul*. We can note that this stem is used both in the l-value and in the r-value of the WHERE expression. In fact, this query requires nesting and indeed the categorizing algorithm needs to be recursive. This stem is classified both as a selection oriented stem for the outer query, and as a projection oriented one for the inner query (note that it requires aggregation, handled when generating the SELECT clause set).

Finally we will introduce one last example to clarify Section 3.5. While with the other examples it is straightforward to compile the FROM clause, since the other clauses refer to the same table, when we deal with columns belonging to different tables things get complicated. Take question *"What are the capitals states bordering Texas?"*) and its associated query SELECT capital FROM ... WHERE border = 'Texas'. How can we fill in the dots in the FROM clause? Fields *capital* and *border* belong respectively to tables *state* and *border_info*. Form the database catalog, we learn that these two tables are connected via the foreign key *state_name* and so the final $\mathcal{F}$ will include the following join: state JOIN border_info on state.state_name = border_info.state_name.

3.1   Optimizing the Dependency List

As introduced in Section 2.1, we don't need all grammatical relations provided in output by the Stanford Dependency parser. For this reason before preprocessing the list of dependencies we need to prune the useless ones and remove from *gov*ernors and *dep*endents the appended number (indicating the position of the word in question q). Then, *gov*s and *dep*s are reduced to stems (using the Porter stemmer[1]).

In order to disambiguate the sense of the stems that do not appear in metadata but could match with it, we create a list of synonyms using off-the-shelf resources (like Wordnet and similarity measures) combined with our internal knowledge (represented by database constraints). Using this list we can substitute certain stems with their stemmed synonyms.

The resulting SDC_q is optimized to be processed by the next step. An example showing $SDC_{q_1}^{opt}$ with respect to the original SDC_{q_1} introduced in Section 2.1 can be found in Table 1.

3.2   Categorizing Stems

Before building $\mathcal{S}$ and $\mathcal{W}$ sets we need to identify those stems that are projection and/or selection oriented. Those stems will be added respectively to Π and/or

---

[1] http://tartarus.org/martin/PorterStemmer/

Table 1. Categorizing stems into projection and/or selection oriented sets

(1)$root$(ROOT, are),	$\Pi = \{\text{capital, state}\}$
(2)$nsubj$(are, capital),	$\Sigma = \{\text{are}\} \Rightarrow \Sigma = \phi$
(3)$prep\_of$(capital, state),	
(4)$nsubj$(border, state),	$\Pi' = \{\text{state, border}\}$
(5)$rcmod$(state, border),	$\Sigma' = \{\text{border, state}\}$
(6)$advmod$(populat, most),	
(7)$amod$(state, populat),	$\Pi'' = \{\text{most, populat, state}\}$
(8)$dobj$(border, state)	$\Sigma'' = \phi$

Σ categories according to the following rules. For each grammatical relation $rel(gov,dep)$ in SDC_q^{opt}:

1. If it is $ROOT$, dep is the key to populate $\mathcal{W}$ so add it to Σ and remove the relation from SDC_q^{opt}. This stem can be an auxiliary verb, e.g., *is, are, has, have* and so on. It is useless to build the arguments of the queries but it could be used transitively to add other stems[2].

2. If it starts with *nsubj*, check if $gov \in \Sigma$. If not (because there isn't any $ROOT$ relation) add gov to Σ. Then add dep to Π and remove rel from SDC_q^{opt}, otherwise keep it, since it could be a subject related to a subordinate (we will need it in the recursive steps).

3. If it starts with *prep* or it ends with *obj*, we used it to create conditions (possibly involving nesting):
   - check if $gov \in \Pi$. If not (because no $ROOT$ or *nsubj* relations were found so far) add gov to Π.
   - Then add dep to Σ if there is not any *table.column* like [3] $gov.dep$. Otherwise, also add dep to Π and remove rel from SDC_q^{opt}.

4. If it ends with *mod*, it implies that dep is a modificator of gov, so they should be paired together: if $gov \in \Sigma$ add dep to Σ and if $gov \in \Pi$ add dep to Π and remove rel from SDC_q^{opt}. This should be done only if dep is not a superlative (i.e. doesn't end with -st). The non-removed relations will be taken into account in the recursive step, adding both dep and gov to Π.

5. If none of the above rules can be applied, iterate the algorthm recursively building Π' and Σ', Π'' and Σ'' and so on, until SDC_q^{opt} is empty.

In order to show how these steps are used to build projection and/or selection oriented sets from which we generate $\mathcal{S}$ and $\mathcal{W}$, let us consider the list of optimized dependencies $SDC_{q_1}^{opt}$ in Table 1.

---

[2] Stems of 3 or less characters would introduce too much noise in retrieving matching strings, so they will be eliminated in an additional step 6. Useful words like *in, of, not, or, and* are embedded in relation abbreviations when collapsing dependencies.

[3] We query metadata seeking for something similar to gov as a table and to dep as a column, i.e. we search for table names using π_{table_name} $(\sigma_{table\_name \cong dep \wedge column\_name \cong gov}(IS.Columns))$. For brevity we use the symbol $s_1 \cong s_2$ for s_2 substring of s_1, i.e. s_1 LIKE "%s_2%".

At the first iteration we use $ROOT$ to add *are* to Σ, then we also exploit it to add *capital* and include *state* to Π as soon as we check that there is an occurrence `state.capital` in IS. At this point these three relations have been deleted from $SDC_{q_1}^{opt}$ obtaining $SDC_{q_1}^{opt\prime}$ used in the next iteration. Note that since *are* is a short stem, it should be deleted from Σ.

At the second iteration (first recursion step) we don't have a $ROOT$ relation so we use *nsubj* to add add *border* to Σ' and *state* to Π'. Since with *rcmod* we find an occurrence `border.state_name` in IS, *border* is added also to Π. At this point, seeking through the end of the list we discard *dobj* because even if *border* $\in \Pi'$ we do not find `state.border` in IS, so these other three relations are deleted from $SDC_{q_1}^{opt\prime}$ obtaining $SDC_{q_1}^{opt\prime\prime}$ for the last iteration.

In the third iteration we have $SDC_{q_1}^{opt\prime\prime}$ composed by two *mod* relations, so we add all stems to Π'' and delete their associated relations from the list.

3.3   Building the SELECT Clauses Set

Once we have identified the set Π of projection-oriented stems, we can use it to search in metadata all the fields that could match with them. The generation process for S is described by the following generative grammar.

$S \rightarrow$ AGGR '(' FIELD ')' | FIELD
AGGR $\rightarrow$ max | min | sum | count | avg
FIELD $\rightarrow$ TAB.COL
TAB $\in \bigcup^{x \in \Pi} \pi_{table\_name}(\sigma_{table\_name \cong x}(\text{IS.Tables}))$
COL $\in \bigcup^{x \in \Pi} \pi_{column\_name}(\sigma_{column\_name \cong x}(\text{IS.Columns}))$

With each element of S, we also associate a weight w_i, calculated according to the procedure described in Section 4.3 (we will discuss it later). For example, considering the IS scheme in Figure 1, the SELECT clauses originated from Π of Table 1 are shown in Fig. 3. Note that the superscript numbers indicate the weight associated with each statement.

$$S = \left\{ state.capital^3, state.state\_name^2, border\_info.state\_name^1, ... \right\}$$
$$S' = \{ border\_info.state\_name^3, border\_info.border^2, state.state\_name^2, ... \}$$
$$S'' = \left\{ max(state.population)^4, max(city.population)^3, state.population^3, ... \right\}$$

Fig. 3. A subset of SELECT clauses for q_1

3.4   Building the WHERE Clauses Set

Before generating WHERE clauses, the selection-oriented set of stems Σ should be divided into two distinct sets: Σ_L and Σ_R.

The set Σ_L contains stems that find their matching in IS and allow us to build the set of left-hand side expressions $\mathcal{W}_L \rightarrow \text{FIELD}^{w_i}$, where FIELD is defined above and computed with Σ_L in place of Π (w_i is its associated weight).

For the remaining stems $\Sigma_R = \Sigma - \Sigma_L$ we search for a match in the database: $\forall col \in IS.Columns$, $\forall tab \in IS.Tables$, generate

$\mathcal{W}_R = \{x | \pi_{count(*)} (\sigma_{col \cong x}(Geoquery.tab)) >= 0\}$.

Then, in order to build the WHERE clause set, $\mathcal{W}$, $\forall e_L \in \mathcal{W}_L$, $\forall e_R \in \mathcal{W}_R$ we first generate basic expressions $expr = e_L \ OP \ _R$ and combine them by means of conjunctions and negations (see Section 2.2), keeping only those expressions $expr$ such that the execution of $\pi_{count(*)} (\sigma_{expr}(table))$ does not lead to an error for at least a *table* in the database.

To understand how it works, let us introduce a new example question q_2: "*what are the capitals of states bordering New York?*". The $SDC^{opt}_{q_2}$ is similar to $SDC^{opt}_{q_1}$ except for the last three relations. Row (6) disappears while rows (7) and (8) are replaced by *amod*(york, new) and *dobj*(border, york), leading to $\Sigma' = \{$border, new, york$\}$. This set is split into $\Sigma'_L = \{$border$\}$ and $\Sigma'_R = \{$new, york$\}$.

We build $\mathcal{W}'_L = \{border\_info.border^3, border\_info.state\_name^2\}$ and $\mathcal{W}'_R = \{'new\ york'^2, 'new\ mexico'^1, 'new\ jersey'^1, 'newark'^1\}$. Finally we generate the set of possible valid conditions and their weights:

$\mathcal{W} = \{border\_info.border = 'new\ york'^5, border\_info.state\_name = 'new\ york'^4, ...\}$.

Anyway, the set Σ_R could happen to be empty. For example, when the WHERE condition requires nesting: in this case e_R will be the whole subquery (e.g. Σ' in Table 1). It could be the case that also Σ_L is empty. In fact a query without a WHERE clause is valid (e.g. Σ'' in Table 1). In any case, even if there are no selection-based stems, $\mathcal{W}$ may not be empty (e.g. Σ in Table 1). Taking into account all tables and columns we can get more conditions: $\mathcal{W}^*_R = \{tab.col$ such that $tab \in \pi_{table\_name}(IS.Columns)$ and $col \in \pi_{column\_name}(IS.Columns)\}$.

3.5   Building the FROM Clauses Set

The generation of the FROM clause $\mathcal{F}$ is straightforward given $\mathcal{S}$ and $\mathcal{W}$. This set will contain all tables to which clauses in $\mathcal{S}$ and $\mathcal{W}$ refer, enriched by pairwise joins.

As stated before, this information can be found running SQL queries over IS exploiting metadata stored in table KEY_COLUMN_USAGE (in short, K; see Figure 2). This table identifies all columns in the current databases that are restricted by some unique, primary key, or foreign key constraint. That is, for each usage of foreign key column in the table, we can determine how many aggregate table columns match that column usage. First, we extract tables appearing in $\mathcal{S}$ and $\mathcal{W}$ (i.e. words ending with dot), creating a set F. At the beginning $\mathcal{F}=F$. Then $\forall t_1, t_2 \in F \ \pi_{col\_name, ref\_col\_name}(\sigma_{table\_name=t_1 \wedge ref\_table\_name=t_2}(IS.K))$ retrieves c_1, c_2 to perform the: join $^{t_1 \bowtie t_2}_{c_1 = c_2}$. In this way $\mathcal{F}$ in enriched whit the two-table join t_1 join t_2 on $t_1.c_1 = t_2.c_2$. In addition we can allow for more distant joins by finding an intermediate table useful to link two tables that are not directly referencing each other. This can be done performing a complex join between two instances of KEYS with multiple conditions, but due to for lack of space this can not be illustrated here.

With respect to our example with question q_1 and its SELECT clauses shown in Figure 3, the set of FROM clauses is:

$\mathcal{F}' = \{state, border, state\ join\ border\ on state.state\_name = border\_info.border, ...\}$.

Note that there are no weights associated with FROM clauses because it is not possible to backtrack how many stems made each table appear in $\mathcal{F}$.

4   Generating Queries

In the previous section we saw how to create building blocks for queries starting from a question q. These elements should be paired together in a smart way to generate the set of queries that possibly answer q. This pairing is obtained by creating the Cartesian product between clauses sets from which non-valid, redundant and meaningless clauses are deleted. We use a weighting scheme to order the most probable correct candidate queries.

4.1   Clause Cartesian Product

In order to find possible answering queries we generate the set $\mathcal{A} = \{\mathcal{S} \times \mathcal{F} \times \mathcal{W}\} \cup \{\mathcal{S} \times \mathcal{F}\}$. Given that at least one such query exists there should be one pairing $\langle s, f, w \rangle \in \mathcal{A}$, such that the execution of SELECT s FROM f [WHERE w] retrieve the correct answer. Given that each clause set contains on average up to ten items, this product can result in a very huge set. Thus, when generating all pairings some preliminary conditions are verified, e.g. tables appearing in SELECT and WHERE clauses should appear in the FROM clause as well, otherwise the execution of that query will fail. This avoids generating incorrect queries and wasting time trying to execute them.

To give a simple example, we illustrate in Figure 4 some generated clauses for the question q_2 , together with possible pairings. The pairing $\langle s_1, f_1, w_1 \rangle$ is not correct: it leads to the MySQL error Unknown table: border_info.

4.2   Pruning Useless Queries

Once the set $\mathcal{A}$ of all valid pairings is built, we additionally prune some of them which are not useful. For example, meaningless queries project the same field compared to a value in the selection (e.g. the pairing $\langle s_3, f_2, w_2 \rangle$ answers the question "Which state is New York?" and is clearly useless).

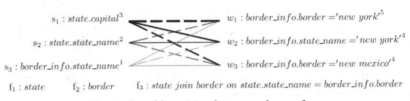

$s_1 : state.capital^3$ $w_1 : border\_info.border = 'new\ york'^5$

$s_2 : state.state\_name^2$ $w_2 : border\_info.state\_name = 'new\ york'^4$

$s_3 : border\_info.state\_name^1$ $w_3 : border\_info.border = 'new\ mexico'^4$

$f_1 : state$ $f_2 : border$ $f_3 : state\ join\ border\ on\ state.state\_name = border\_info.border$

Fig. 4. Possible pairing between clauses for q_2

Moreover there could be redundant queries that, if optimized, allow us to remove duplicates in the set, reducing its cardinality. For example, the pairing $\langle s_2, f_3, w_1 \rangle$ requires the columns *state.state_name* and *border_info.border* to be the same, so w_2 would select the same rows of w_2'(i.e. *state.state_name= 'new york'*), but this means that table *border_info* is no longer used and this pairing is equivalent to $\langle s_2, f_1, w_2' \rangle$ which, as said above, is meaningless.

4.3 Weighting Scheme

As introduced in the previous sections, we weigh each clause in $\mathcal{S}$ and $\mathcal{W}$ by counting how many stems in the original question originated that clause.

In particular, for the SELECT clause, if there is a table that matches with a stem, its weight is +2 while the matching with columns weighs +1 (common stems between table and column are not valid). Superlatives matching with aggregation operators count as +1.

For the WHERE clause, a weight is computed in the same way as for the left-hand side of the conditions and a +1 is added for each matching value in the right-hand side. In addition when dealing with nested queries, the WHERE clause inherits also the weight of the nested query.

The FROM clauses are not associated with weights. However, we will take into account how many joins are involved when ordering queries with the same weight.

When pairing clauses the total weight is obtained just summing up the weight of its components, and it is used to order the final set $\bar{A}$ of possible useful queries from the most to the least probable.

Figure 4 highlights this *probabilistic* score (obtained by the heuristic one by normalization) through the thickness of connection lines. Dashed lines illustrate pruned queries. The final ordered set answering q_2 is the following one:
$\bar{A}=\{\langle s_1, f_3, w_2 \rangle^7, \langle s_3, f_2, w_1 \rangle^6, \langle s_2, f_3, w_2 \rangle^6, \langle s_1, f_1 \rangle^3, \langle s_2, f_1 \rangle^2, \langle s_3, f_2 \rangle^1\}$.
From the pairing with highest weight we derive the answering query, that is:
`SELECT state.capital FROM state join border on state.state_name =border_info.border WHERE border_info.state_name='new york'`.

It is worth noting that more then a query can have the same weight. To deal with that, we implemented a comparator that privileges queries involving less joins and embed the most referenced table (e.g. `state` in the case of GEO-QUERY). See, for example, the order of the second and third pairings in $\bar{A}$: they have been swapped since f_3 contains a join while f_2 doesn't.

5   Kernel Methods for Ranking Question/Query Mapping

Once an initial rank of the candidate SQL queries has been derived, we can rely on machine learning methods to improve the probability of finding the correct answer in the top position. The need of designing suitable representations of the question and query pairs makes this operation quite complex. For this purpose, we rely on kernel methods.

5.1   Kernel Methods

In kernel-based machines, both learning and classification algorithms only depend on the inner product between instances. In several cases this can be efficiently and implicitly computed by kernel functions by exploiting the following dual formulation: $\sum_{i=1..l} y_i \alpha_i \phi(o_i) \phi(o) + b = 0$, where o_i and o are two objects, ϕ is a mapping from the objects to feature vectors $\boldsymbol{x_i}$ and $\phi(o_i)\phi(o) = K(o_i, o)$ is a kernel function implicitly defining such mapping. In case of structural kernels, K determines the shape of the substructures that describe the objects above.

In the following section, we are going to first propose a structural representation of the question and query pairs, then we will illustrate the Syntactic Tree Kernel (STK) [2], which computes the number of syntactic tree fragments. In the last subsection we will show how to engineer new kernels from them, while the reranking kernel is presented in Sec. 5.5

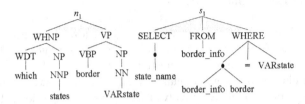

Fig. 5. Question/Query Syntactic trees

5.2   Representing Question and Queries Pairs

In Data Mining and Information Retrieval the so-called bag-of-words (BOW) has been shown to be effective to represent textual documents, e.g. [12,6]. However, in case of questions and queries, we deal with small textual objects in which the semantic content is expressed by means of few words and poorly reliable probability distributions. In these conditions the use of syntactic representation improves BOW and should be always used.

Therefore, in addition to BOW, we represent questions and queries using their syntactic trees, as shown in Figure 5: for questions (a) we used the Charniak's syntactic parser [1] while for queries (b) we implemented an ad-hoc SQL parser. The latter builds a SQL parse tree for each query following its syntactic derivation according to MySQL grammar. The grammar has been slightly modified to accommodate the usage of the symbol • for the production of *items* in the SELECT clause and in WHERE conditions. In such an SQL tree, the internal nodes are only the SQL keywords of the query plus the special symbol • whereas the leaves are names of tables and columns of the database, category variables or operators. Note that, although we eliminated comma and dot from the grammar, it is still possible to obtain the original SQL query, by just performing a preorder traversal of the tree. The above structures can be represented in a learning algorithm using the kernel described in the next section.

5.3   Syntactic Tree Kernels (STK)

Convolution tree kernels [2] compute the similarity between two trees T_1 and T_2 by counting the common sub-trees, without enumerating the whole fragment space. In more detail, let N_1 and N_2 be the set of nodes in T_1 and T_2, respectively. Moreover, let $I_i(n)$ be an indicator variable that is 1 if subtree i is rooted at n and 0 otherwise. Then the convolution kernel K over $T1$ and $T2$ is computed as:

$$STK(T1, T2) = \sum_{n_1 \in N_1, n_2 \in N_2} \Delta(n_1, n_2) \tag{4}$$

where

$$\Delta(n_1, n_2) = \sum_{n_1 \in N_1} \sum_{n_2 \in N_2} \sum_i I_i(n_1) I_i(n_2)$$

is computed efficiently using the following recursive definition:

- If the production rules[4] at n_1 and n_2 are different, then $\Delta(n_1, n_2) = 0$.
- If the production rules at n_1 and n_2 are the same and n_1 and n_2 are pre-terminals, then $\Delta(n_1, n_2) = \lambda$.
- If the production rules at n_1 and n_2 are the same and n_1 and n_2 are not pre-terminals, then:

$$\Delta(n_1, n_2) = \lambda \prod_{j=1}^{nc(n1)} (1 + \Delta(ch(n_1, j)), ch(n_2, j))$$

where $nc(n_1)$ is the number of children of n_1 in the tree and the j-th children of node n_i is denoted by $ch(n_i, j)$ (note that $nc(n_1) = nc(n_2)$ since the production rule is the same). λ ($0 < \lambda < 1$) is a decay factor to make the kernel less variable with respect to tree-fragment sizes.

5.4   Kernel Combination for Pairs

We need to represent the members of a pair and their interdependencies. For this purpose, given two kernel functions, $k_1(.,.)$ and $k_2(.,.)$, and two pairs, $p_1 = \langle n_1, s_1 \rangle$ and $p_2 = \langle n_2, s_2 \rangle$, a first approximation is given by summing the kernels applied to the components: $K(p_1, p_2) = k_1(n_1, n_2) + k_2(s_1, s_2)$. This kernel will produce the union of the feature spaces of questions and queries. A more effective kernel is the product $k(n_1, n_2) \times k(s_1, s_2)$, since it generates pairs of fragments, which are member of the Cartesian product of kernel spaces of the questions and queries. As additional feature and kernel engineering, we also exploit the ability of the polynomial kernel to add feature conjunctions. By simply applying the function $(1 + K(p_1, p_2))^d$, we can generate conjunction up to d features. Thus, we can obtain tree fragment conjunctions and conjunctions of pairs of tree fragments.

The next section will show how to use such kernels for an SVM-based reranker.

---

[4] In a syntactic tree a node with its children correspond to a production rule of the grammar that generated it.

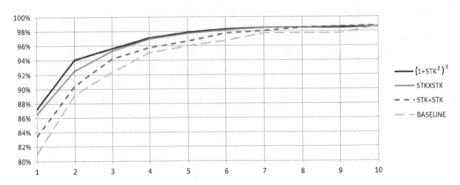

Fig. 6. Recall of the correct answer within different k positions of the system rank

5.5   Preference Reranker

Our reranking model consists in learning to select the best candidate from a given candidate set. In order to use SVMs for training a reranker, we applied the Preference Kernel Method [13]. In the Preference Kernel approach, the reranking problem – learning to pick the correct candidate h_1 from a candidate set $\{h_1, \ldots, h_k\}$ – is reduced to a binary classification problem by creating *pairs*: positive training instances $\langle h_1, h_2 \rangle, \ldots, \langle h_1, h_k \rangle$ and negative instances $\langle h_2, h_1 \rangle, \ldots, \langle h_k, h_1 \rangle$. This training set can then be used to train a binary classifier. At classification time, pairs are not formed (since the correct candidate is not known), while, the standard one-versus-all binarization method is still applied.

The kernels are then engineered to implicitly represent the *differences* between the objects in the pairs. If we have a valid kernel K over the candidate space $\mathcal{T}$, we can construct a preference kernel P_K over the space of pairs $\mathcal{T} \times \mathcal{T}$ as follows: $P_K(x, y) =$

$$P_K(\langle x_1, x_2 \rangle, \langle y_1, y_2 \rangle) = K(x_1, y_1) + \\ K(x_2, y_2) - K(x_1, y_2) - K(x_2, y_1), \tag{5}$$

where $x, y \in \mathcal{T} \times \mathcal{T}$. It is easy to show that P_K is also a valid Mercer's kernel. This makes it possible to use kernel methods to train the reranker. The several kernels defined in the previous section can be used in place of K^5 in Eq. 5.

6   The Experiments

We ran several experiments to evaluate the accuracy of our approach for automatic generation and selection of correct SQL queries from NL questions. We experimented with a well-known dataset GeoQuery developed in order to study semantic parsing.

---

[5] More precisely, we also multiply K for the inverse of rank position.

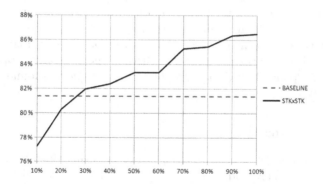

Fig. 7. Learning curve comparison between simple answer generator and the reranking model using the STK × STK kernel

6.1 Setup

To learn the reranker, we used SVM-Light-TK[6], which extends the SVM-Light optimizer [6] with tree kernels. i.e. Syntactic Tree Kernel (STK) as described in Section 5. We modeled many different combinations described in the next section. We used the default parameters, i.e. the cost and trade-off parameters = 1 (for normalized kernels) and $\lambda = 0.4$ (see Sec. 4).

To generate the set of possible SQL queries we applied our algorithm described in Section 3 to GEOQUERIES[7] corpus. We started from a set of 700 NL questions[8]. Thanks to our generative algorithm we discovered and fixed all errors and inconsistencies in SQL queries, except for 3 cases that still lead to a MySQL error. Indeed, since we can't test the correctness of our generated query (without a result set to compare with) we considered a subset of 697 pairs.

6.2 Generative Results

Given a question from GeoQuery, our algorithm was able to generate a correct SQL query in the first 25 in 95.3% of the cases. This also means that our system cannot answer to 33 questions. This is due to (1) empty clauses set $\mathcal{S}$ and/or $\mathcal{W}$, for example, "*How many square kilometers in the us?*" does not contain any useful stem; and (2) from mismatching nested queries, for example, "*Count the states which have elevations lower than what alabama has*" contains an implicit reference to a missing piece of question. In addition there are ambiguous questions like "*Which states does the colorado?*" from which we retrieve an incomplete dependency set.

For all remaining questions from which we succeed in generating an ordered list of possible queries, we find that the query on top of the list retrieves the

---

[6] http://disi.unitn.it/~moschitt/Tree-Kernel.htm
[7] Available at http://www.cs.utexas.edu/ ml/geo.html
[8] This are the first 700 questions of the 880 ones that Mooney's group [14] paired with logical formulas in Prolog and that Popescu et al. [10] manually converted into SQL.

correct result set in 82% of the cases. For the other questions, it can be found within the first 10 generated answers for 99% of the questions (once the 33 questions above have been removed). This can be observed in Figure 6, which plots the Recall (of the correct question) curve of the generative approach, i.e., the baseline. As pointed out in the graphic, the right query is found among the first three in 93% of the cases.

6.3   Reranking Results

Figure 6 also shows the plot for different rerankers using the following kernels: STK+STK, STK×STK and $(1+STK×STK)^2$, which provide better rankings (the first STK is applied to the question parse trees whereas the second STK is applied to the query derivation tree). For example, the latter kernel retrieved the correct answers 94% of times by only using the first two answers.

To better evaluate the results of our rerankers, we applied standard 10-fold cross validation and measure the average Recall and Std Dev. of selecting a query for each question. The results for different kernel models for reranking are reported in Table 2. The first column of Table 2 lists kernel combination by means of product and sum between pairs of basic kernels used for the question and the query, respectively. The other columns show the percentage of questions for which we found at least 1 correct answer in the top @X positions (average Recall@X over 10 folds ± Std. Dev).

The results are rather exciting since they compare favorably with the state-of-the-art. The best system on this datasets was designed in [15] and shows a Precision of 96.3% and a Recall of 79.3%, for an f-measure of 86.9%, while our system shows a Precision of 82.8% and a Recall of 87.2%, for an f-measure of 85.0% (when we include the 33 missing questions in the evaluation). Two main facts should be noted:

- our system performs just 2 points less than the system designed in [15] but it does not need any hand-crafted manual resource, i.e., the semantic trees manually designed in [15] for each question, and it is very simple to implement.
- unlike it has been done in previous work, we can also provide multiple ranked answers. If we select the first n candidates, we highly increasing the Recall

Table 2. Kernel combination recall (± Std. Dev) for GEO dataset

Combination	Rec@1	Rec@2	Rec@3	Rec@4	Rec@5
NO RERANKING	81.4±5.8	87.6±3.8	90.8±3.1	94.0±2.4	95.0±2.0
STK + STK	83.5±3.6	90.4±3.5	94.2±2.9	95.8±2.0	96.7±1.7
STK × STK	86.5±4.0	92.6±3.7	95.3±3.2	97.0±1.8	97.7±1.4
$(1+STK^2)^2$	87.2±3.9	94.1±3.4	95.6±2.7	97.1±1.9	97.9±1.4
BOW × STK	86.7±4.1	92.1±3.2	95.6±2.5	97.1±1.4	97.6±1.2

of the correct answers, e.g., within the first 2 we have a f-measure of 90% (considering the 33 missing questions).

Other closely related work, e.g., [4], suggests that lower results than ours can be obtained using different approaches. These rely either on semantic grammar specified by an expert user [9], or on enriching the information contained in the pairs [10] and implementing ad-hoc rules in a semantic parser [7,11]. Our system instead, requires no intervention since the database metadata already contains all the needed data.

Finally, we report the learning curve of one basic reranker in Figure 7, showing how recall of STK×STK increases for larger training sets. The plot reveals that as soon as we provide a reasonable percentage of training data (25% of the available data corresponding to 9 folds of 700 questions – one fold is used for testing) for reranking, the model improves on the baseline.

The main contribution of this research consist in the fact that given a NL question we can generate a set of mapping SQL queries. Moreover if we can rely on a relatively small set of correct pairs of questions and queries to train a SVM classifier, we are able to re-rank the set of generated pairs to select the correct one with a fairly high accuracy.

7 Conclusions and Future Work

In this paper, we have approached the question answering task of implementing a NL interface to databases by automatically generating SQL queries based on grammatical relations and matching metadata. To our knowledge, the underlying idea that we have proposed to build and combine clauses sets is novelty. Additionally, we are firstly experimented with a preference reranking kernel, which is able to boost the accuracy of our generative model.

Given the high accuracy, the simplicity and the practical usefulness of our approach, (e.g., we can generate the correct question in the first 5 candidates in 95% of the cases), we believe that our methods can be successfully used in the future for real-world applications.

In the future we plan to experiment with datasets in different domains (e.g. ATIS corpus). Moreover, given that current challenges in Semantic Web tackle similar problem [5] (scaling question answering approaches to Linked Data, i.e. Question Answering over Linked Data), it would be interesting to apply our algorithms to semantic search and question answering over RDF data.

References

1. Charniak, E.: A maximum-entropy-inspired parser. In: Proceedings of NAACL 2000 (2000)
2. Collins, M., Duffy, N.: New ranking algorithms for parsing and tagging: Kernels over discrete structures, and the voted perceptron. In: Proceedings of ACL 2002 (2002)

3. Garcia-Molina, H., Ullman, J.D., Widom, J.: Database Systems: The Complete Book, 2nd edn. Prentice Hall Press, Upper Saddle River (2008)
4. Giordani, A., Moschitti, A.: Corpora for automatically learning to map natural language questions into sql queries. In: Proceedings of LREC 2010, Valletta, Malta. European Language Resources Association (ELRA) (May 2010)
5. Granberg, J., Minock, M.: A natural language interface over the musicbrainz database. In: Proceedings of the 1st Workshop on Question Answering over Linked Data (QALD-1): Co-located with the 8th Extended Semantic Web Conference, pp. 38–43 (2011), QC 20120413
6. Joachims, T.: Making large-scale SVM learning practical. In: Schölkopf, B., Burges, C., Smola, A. (eds.) Advances in Kernel Methods (1999)
7. Kate, R.J., Mooney, R.J.: Using string-kernels for learning semantic parsers. In: Proceedings of the 21st ICCL and 44th Annual Meeting of the ACL, Sydney, Australia, pp. 913–920. Association for Computational Linguistics (July 2006)
8. MacCartney, B., de Marneffe, M.-C., Manning, C.D.: Generating typed dependency parses from phrase structure parses. In: Proceedings LREC 2006 (2006)
9. Minock, M., Olofsson, P., Näslund, A.: Towards building robust natural language interfaces to databases. In: Kapetanios, E., Sugumaran, V., Spiliopoulou, M. (eds.) NLDB 2008. LNCS, vol. 5039, pp. 187–198. Springer, Heidelberg (2008)
10. Popescu, A.-M., Etzioni, O.A., Kautz, H.A.: Towards a theory of natural language interfaces to databases. In: Proceedings of the 2003 International Conference on Intelligent User Interfaces, Miami. Association for Computational Linguistics (2003)
11. Ruwanpura, S.: Sq-hal: Natural language to sql translator
12. Salton, G.: Recent trends in automatic information retrieval. In: Proceedings of the 9th Annual International ACM SIGIR Conference on Research and Development in Information Retrieval, SIGIR 1986, Pisa, Italy, September 8-10, pp. 1–10. ACM (1986)
13. Shen, L., Joshi, A.K.: An SVM-based voting algorithm with application to parse reranking. In: Proceedings of the Seventh Conference on Natural Language Learning at HLT-NAACL 2003, pp. 9–16 (2003)
14. Tang, L.R., Mooney, R.J.: Using multiple clause constructors in inductive logic programming for semantic parsing. In: Flach, P.A., De Raedt, L. (eds.) ECML 2001. LNCS (LNAI), vol. 2167, pp. 466–477. Springer, Heidelberg (2001)
15. Zettlemoyer, L.S., Collins, M.: Learning to map sentences to logical form: Structured classification with probabilistic categorial grammars. In: UAI, pp. 658–666 (2005)

Assessment of Software Testing and Quality Assurance in Natural Language Processing Applications and a Linguistically Inspired Approach to Improving It

K. Bretonnel Cohen*, Lawrence E. Hunter, and Martha Palmer

Computational Bioscience Program,
University of Colorado School of Medicine,
Aurora, Colorado, USA
Department of Linguistics,
University of Colorado at Boulder,
Boulder, Colorado, USA

Abstract. Significant progress has been made in addressing the scientific challenges of biomedical text mining. However, the transition from a demonstration of scientific progress to the production of tools on which a broader community can rely requires that fundamental software engineering requirements be addressed. In this paper we characterize the state of biomedical text mining software with respect to software testing and quality assurance. Biomedical natural language processing software was chosen because it frequently specifically claims to offer production-quality services, rather than just research prototypes.

We examined twenty web sites offering a variety of text mining services. On each web site, we performed the most basic software test known to us and classified the results. Seven out of twenty web sites returned either bad results or the worst class of results in response to this simple test. We conclude that biomedical natural language processing tools require greater attention to software quality.

We suggest a linguistically motivated approach to granular evaluation of natural language processing applications, and show how it can be used to detect performance errors of several systems and to predict overall performance on specific equivalence classes of inputs.

We also assess the ability of linguistically-motivated test suites to provide good software testing, as compared to large corpora of naturally-occurring data. We measure code coverage and find that it is considerably higher when even small structured test suites are utilized than when large corpora are used.

1 Introduction

Biomedical natural language processing tools and data generated by their application are beginning to gain widespread use in biomedical research. Significant

---

* Corresponding author.

A. Moschitti and B. Plank (Eds.): EternalS 2013, CCIS 379, pp. 77–90, 2013.

progress has been made recently in addressing the scientific challenges of creating computer programs that can properly handle the complexities of human language. However, the transition from a demonstration of scientific progress to the production of tools on which a broader community can depend requires that fundamental software engineering requirements be addressed. Software for medical devices has the benefit of explicit quality assurance requirements per Section 201(h) of the Federal Food, Drug, and Cosmetic Act; Title 21 of the Code of Federal Regulations Part 820; and 61 Federal Register 52602 [8] (p. 7). However, unless it is embedded in a medical device, biomedical natural language processing software is not currently subject to federal quality assurance requirements.

This paper represents the first attempt to characterize the state of one portion of the diverse world of computational bioscience software, specifically biomedical natural language processing applications, with respect to software testing and quality assurance. We assay a broad range of biomedical natural language processing services that are made available via web sites for evidence of quality assurance processes. Our findings suggest that at the current time, software testing and quality assurance are lacking in the community that produces biomedical natural language processing tools. For the tool consumer, this finding should come as a note of caution.

2   Approach to Assessing the State of Natural Language Processing Applications with Respect to Software Testing and Quality Assurance

We looked at twenty web sites offering a variety of text-mining-related services. In the body of this work, we never identify them by name: following the tradition in natural language processing, we do not want to punish people for making their work freely available. Our purpose is not to point fingers—indeed, one of our own services is every bit as lacking in most or all of the measures that we describe below as any. Rather, our goal is to allow the community to make a realistic assessment of the state of the art with respect to software testing and quality assurance for biomedical natural language processing systems, with the hope of stimulating a healthy change.

The claim to have produced a useful tool is a commonplace in the biomedical natural language processing literature. The explicitly stated motivation for much work in the field is to assist in the understanding of disease or of life, *not* to advance the state of computer science or of understanding of natural (i.e., human) language. (In this, the biomedical natural language processing community differs from the mainstream NLP community, which at least in theory is motivated by a desire to investigate hypotheses about NLP or about natural language, not to produce tools.) Software is widely known to be characterized by "bugs," or undesired behaviors—[15] reviews a wide range of studies that suggest an industry average of error rates of 1 to 25 bugs per thousand lines of code in a wide variety of types of software, and a Food and Drug Administration analysis of 3,140 medical device recalls in the 1990s concluded that 7.7% of them (242/3,140) were due to software errors [8] (p. 7). Given the stated intent to provide "mission-critical" tools to doctors and researchers, one might expect due diligence with regard to the quality of software artifacts to be a commonplace in the biomedical natural language processing community and an established subfield of its research milieu. Surprisingly, that is not the case: on the widest imaginable definition of quality assurance, there are fewer than a dozen published studies on quality assurance for biomedical natural language processing software, despite the high (and rapidly growing) level of activity in the biomedical natural language processing area reported in [24] and reviewed in work such as [25]. Given the apparently urgent need for biomedical natural language processing tools that many papers claim in an introductory paragraph citing the latest count of papers in PubMed/MEDLINE, it seems plausible that although researchers in the area *are* exercising due diligence with respect to the artifacts that they produce, they simply are not taking the time to do research on quality assurance per se. We assayed the extent to which this might be the case, and report the results here.

3   Methods and Results for Assessing Natural Language Processing Applications with Respect to Software Testing and Quality Assurance

Our methodology was simple. We examined 20 web sites that either provide some form of text mining service (e.g. gene name identification or protein-protein interaction extraction) or provide access to the output of text mining (e.g. a text-mining-produced database). On each web site, we tried the most basic software test imaginable. This test, which our experience suggests is probably the first action performed by a typical professional software tester presented with any new application to test, consists of passing the application an empty input. For many web sites, the test consisted of simply hitting the "Submit" button or its equivalent. For some web sites, this was first preceded by clearing sample input from a text box. This is indeed the simplest and most basic software test of which we are aware. We make the following (undoubtedly simplified) assumption: if the system builders paid any attention to software testing and quality assurance at all, they will have run this test; evidence that they tried the test will be that the system responds to a blank input by prompting the user to populate the empty field.

What constitutes an appropriate response to an empty input? We propose that the best response to an empty input where a non-empty input was expected is to give the user helpful feedack—to prompt the user to provide an input. For a GUI-based application, the next-best response is probably Google's strategy—to do nothing, and present the user with the exact same input screen. (For an API, the second-best response may well be to throw an uncaught exception—this has the advantage of making it clear to the programmer that something is amiss.) This second-best response is not necessarily bad.

A bad response would be to return something. For example, we found that in response to an empty input, many systems will return something along the lines of "0 results found". This is bad in that it does not allow the user (or the calling routine) to differentiate between the situation where no results were found because the input is empty and the situation where no results were found because there truly should not have been any results—the user is given no indication whatsoever that anything was amiss with the input in the former case. (A less common phenomenon that we observed was that a system might return results that are clearly invalid if examined by a human. For example, one system returned a table full of SQL error messages when passed an empty input. This may not be a problem when called from a GUI, but if called by an API, the results might not be noticed until much later in the processing pipeline, if at all, and are likely to be difficult to track down to their origin.) Finally, the worst possible response is to return *something that looks like a legitimate response*. For example, one application that we examined returns a perfectly valid-looking list of disease-associated quantitative trait loci (multiple gene locations that contribute to a single physical manifestation) when passed an empty input. This program may seriously mislead an application that calls it.

In total, we examined 23 web sites, selecting them in alphabetical order from a web page that lists biomedical natural language processing applications[1]. Two of them were down completely, and one of them crashed every time that we attempted to use it, whether or not the input field was empty. Table 1 summarizes the results: of the 20 that were operative and did not crash, a full 7/20 returned either the "bad" or the "worst" type of results, and one of those seven returned the worst.

This test assesses the user interface, not the underlying functionality. However, we suspect that the testing applied to the interface that authors use to showcase their work to the world may be better than the testing applied to their underlying application. And, it is certainly the case that this test can reveal real problems with the underlying application, as in the system described above which returned a table of SQL error messages in response to the test.

As a reviewer pointed out, the test is not repeatable—web sites go down, their functionality is changed, and their authors sometimes respond to bug reports. However, the survey captures a snapshot of the state of the biomedical natural language processing world at one point in time, and the general approach is applicable to any application.

4   A Linguistically Motivated Approach to Testing Natural Language Processing Applications

Although the natural language processing community has a long tradition of global evaluation of applications in terms of global metrics like precision, recall, and

---

[1] http://biocreative.sourceforge.net/ bionlp_tools_links.html

Table 1. Summary of behaviors. 7 of 20 sites returned the "bad" or "worst" type of results.

Response type	Sites
Good (prompt or input screen displayed)	13
Bad (invalid-appearing or false 0 returned)	6
Worst (valid-appearing data returned)	1

F-measure, there has been much less work on granular evaluation of the performance of such applications. (In the remainder of the paper, there is a deliberate blurring or mixing of metaphors between what Palmer and Finin have called *glass-box evaluation* (which I refer to as granular evaluation), or fine-grained evaluation of specific linguistic features [18]; and finding errors in performance, or bugs. As will be seen, it is fruitful to blur this distinction.) There has been correspondingly little research on methods for doing so. We describe here a methodology for granular evaluation of the performance of natural language processing applications using techniques from traditional software testing and from linguistics. Software testing conventionally makes use of test suites. A *test suite* is a set of test inputs with known desired outputs that is structured so as to explore the feature space of a specified type of input. Test cases are built by determining the set of features that a type of input might have and the contexts in which those features might be found. For a simple example, a function that takes numbers as inputs might be tested with a test suite that includes integers, real numbers, positive numbers, negative numbers, and zero. Good testing also includes a suite of "dirty" or unexpected inputs—for example, the function that takes numbers as inputs might be passed a null variable, a non-null but empty variable, and letters.

There is a theoretical background for test suite construction. It turns out to be overwhelmingly similar to the formal foundations of linguistics. Indeed, if one examines the table of contents of a book on the theory of software testing (see several listed below) and Partee et al.'s textbook on the formal foundations of linguistics [19], one finds very similar chapters. The table of contents of [19] includes chapters on basic concepts of set theory, relations and functions, properties of relations, basic concepts of logic and formal systems, statement logic, predicate logic, finite automata, formal languages, and Type 3 grammars. Similarly, if we look at the contents of a good book on software testing, we see coverage of set theory [2], graphs and relations [3], logic [2], and automata [2,3,14].

The theoretical similarities between software testing and linguistics turn out to translate into practical methodologies, as well. In particular, the techniques of software testing have much in common with the techniques of descriptive or field linguistics—the specialty of determining the structures and functioning of an unknown language. In the case of software testing, an application is approached by determining the features of inputs and combinations of inputs (both "clean" and "dirty") that an application might be presented with, and constructing test suites to explore this feature space. In field linguistics, an unknown language is approached by constructing questions to be answered about the language that allow us to determine the elements of the language on all levels—phonemic and phonetic (sounds), morphological (word formation), lexicon (words), syntactic (phrasal structure)—and the ways in which they can combine. These questions are formulated in sets called *schedules* that are assembled to elucidate specific aspects of the language, in a procedure known as *scheduled elicitation*. The software tester's test suites have a clear analogue in the "schedules" of the field linguist. Like test suites, schedules include "dirty" data, as well—for example, in studying the syntax of a language, the linguist will test the acceptability of sentences that his or her theory of the language predicts to be ungrammatical. Thus, even though there has not been extensive research into the field of software testing of natural language processing applications, we already have a well-developed methodology available to us for doing so, provided by the techniques of descriptive linguistics.

An example of how the techniques of software testing and descriptive linguistics can be merged in this way is provided in [6]. This paper looked at the problem of testing named entity recognition systems. *Named entity recognition* is the task of finding mentions of items of a specific semantic type in text. Commonly addressed semantic types have been human names, company names, and locations (hence the term "named entity" recognition). [6] looked at the application of named entity recognition to gene names. They constructed a test suite based on analyzing the linguistic characteristics of gene names and the contexts in which they can appear in a sentence. Linguistic characteristics of gene names included orthographic and typographic features on the level of individual characters, such as letter case, the presence or absence of punctuation marks (gene names may contain hyphens, parentheses, and apostrophes), and the presence or absence of numerals. (Gene names and symbols often contain numbers or letters that indicate individual members of a family of genes. For example, the *HSP* family of genes contains the genes *HSP1, HSP2, HSP3,* and *HSP4*.) Morphosyntactic features addressed characteristics of the morpheme or word, such as the presence or absence of participles, the presence or absence of genitives, and the presence or absence of function words. The contextual features included whether or not a gene name was an element of a list, its position in the sentence, and whether or not it was part of an appositive construction. (Gene names can have a dizzying variety of forms, as they may reflect the physical or behavioral characteristics of an organism in which they are mutated, the normal function of the gene when it is not mutated, or conditions with which they are associated. Thus, we see gene names like *pizza* (reflecting the appearance of a fly's brain when the gene is mutated), *heat shock protein 60* (reflecting the function of the gene), and *muscular dystrophy* (reflecting a disease with which the gene is associated). This high range of variability adds greatly to the difficulty of gene name recognition.)

Five different gene name recognition systems were then examined. These features of gene names and features of contexts were sufficient to find errors in every system. One system missed every one-word gene name. One system missed lower-case-initial gene names when they occurred in sentence-initial position. (Sentences in genomics articles can begin with a lower-case letter if they begin with the name of a gene and the mutant form of the gene, commonly named with a lower-case-initial name, is being discussed.) One system only found multi-word gene names if every word of the name was upper-case-initial. One system only found multi-word names if they ended with an alphanumeric modifier (e.g. the gene names *alcohol dehydrogenase 6* or *spindle A*). One system missed all numerals at the right edge of gene names (see preceding example). One system missed names, but not symbols, containing hyphens (catching symbols like *Nat-1* but missing names like the corresponding *N-acetyltransferase 1*). One system missed names containing apostrophes just in the case where they were genitives (catching names like *5' nucleotidase precursor* but missing names like *corneal dystrophy of Bowman's layer type II (Thiel-Behnke)*). Two systems had failures related to the format of Greek letters. One system performed well on symbols but did not recognize any names at all. (Genes typically have both a name, such as *white* or *N-acetyltransferase 1*, and a "symbol," similar to an abbreviation, such as *w* for *white* and *Nat-1* for *N-acetyltransferase*.)

Test suites are effective for granular evaluation of performance, but should not be able to predict global measures such as precision, recall, and F-measure, since the proportions of named entity types in the test suite do not reflect the distribution of those types in naturally occurring data. (In fact, this is one of their advantages—as pointed out by [17], an advantage of test suites is that they limit the redundancy of common entity types and address the scarcity of rare entity types that are observed in naturally occurring data.) However, it was hypothesized that test suites might be able to predict performance on specific equivalence classes of inputs (where an *equivalence class* is a set of inputs that are all expected to test the same functionality and reveal the same bugs; they are similar to what linguists call *natural classes*). To test this hypothesis, the authors built a number of simple test suites, varying only the length of the gene name, letter case, hyphenation, and sentence position. They then ran a single gene name recognition system on all of these test suites. Based on the results obtained from the test suites, they made the following predictions:

1. Recall should be poor for gene names with initial numerals, such as *12-LOX* and *18-wheeler*.
2. Recall should be poor for gene names that contain function words, such as *Pray for elves* and *ken and barbie*.
3. Recall should be poor for upper-case-initial gene names in sentence-medial position.
4. Recall should be poor for 3-character-long symbols.
5. Recall should be good for numeral-final gene names such as *yeast heat shock protein 60*.

The system was then used to process two corpora containing gene names—the BioCreative I corpus [23] and the PMC corpus [22]. Overall performance for the BioCreative I corpus was a precision of 0.65 and recall of 0.68. Overall performance for the PMC corpus was a precision of 0.71 and recall of 0.62.

The performance of the system for the various equivalence classes was as shown in Table 2.

Table 2. Performance on two corpora for the predictable categories [6]

Prediction	BioCreative				
	TP	FP	FN	P	R
1	12	57	17	0.17	0.41
2	0	1	38	0.0	0.0
4	556	278	512	0.67	0.52
5	284	251	72	0.53	0.80
	PubMed Central				
	TP	FP	FN	P	R
1	8	10	0	0.44	1.0
2	1	0	2	1.0	0.33
4	163	64	188	0.72	0.46
5	108	54	46	0.67	0.70

The predictions based on the test suites were almost entirely supported. The single anomaly was the high recall observed on the PMC corpus for prediction 1, where low recall was predicted. In all other cases, the predictions were correct—recall for the equivalence class was predicted to be low for 1, 2, and 4 and it was lower than the recall for the corpus as a whole for these equivalence classes; recall was predicted to be high for 5, and it was higher than the recall for the corpus as a whole for this equivalence class.

It will be noted that there are no results given for prediction 3. This is because it concerns letter case, and letter case had been normalized to lower case in the corpora. This points out again an advantage of test suites—we know that such gene names exist in the literature, but they were not represented in these corpora at all, making the corpora unsuitable for assessing the performance of a system on this type of name.

It should be noted that these findings are significant (in the non-statistical sense of that term) *because of* the small numbers of items in some of the cells, not in spite of it. These details of performance would likely be lost in an evaluation that only assessed precision, recall, and F-measure, and are the difference between finding or missing elusive statements that are of crucial interest to the biologist, perhaps precisely because of their rarity.

5 An Engineering Perspective on the Use of Test Suites versus Corpora

To the extent that testing is considered in the natural language processing community, there is an implicit assumption that the way to test an application is

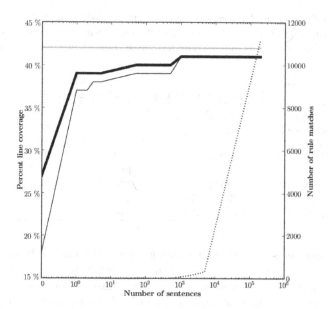

Fig. 1. Increase in percentage of line coverage as increasing amounts of the corpus are processed. The left y axis is the percent coverage. The right y axis is the number of rule matches [7].

by running it on a large corpus. We tested this assumption by measuring code coverage when a natural language processing application was run with a large corpus as its input and with a small structured test suite as its input. The natural language processing application was a semantic parser known as OpenDMAP [11]. It allows free mixing of terminals and non-terminals, and semantically typed phrasal constituents, such as "gene phrases." It has been applied to a variety of information extraction tasks in the biomedical domain and has achieved winning results in two shared tasks [1,9].

Code coverage is a measure of the percentage of code in an application that is executed during the running of a test suite. The goal is to maximize coverage—bugs in code will not be found if the code is not executed. Various kinds of coverage can be measured. *Line coverage* is the percentage of lines of code that have been executed. It is the weakest indicator of code coverage. *Branch coverage* is the percentage of branches within conditionals that have been traversed. It is more informative than line coverage.

The corpus that we employed was the largest biomedical corpus available at the time. It consisted of 3,947,200 words. The test suite that we used was much smaller. It contained altogether 278 test cases constructed by the application developer. He did not monitor code coverage while designing the test suite.

Table 3 (next page) shows the results of running the application on the corpus and on the test suite. As can be seen, the small test suite yielded higher code coverage for every component of the system and every measure of code

Table 3. Application- and package-level coverage statistics using the test suite, the full corpus with the full set of rules, and the full corpus with two reduced sets of rules. The highest value in a row is bolded. The last three columns are intentionally identical [7].

Metric	Functional tests	Corpus, all rules	nominal rules	verbal rules
Overall line coverage	**56%**	41%	41%	41%
Overall branch coverage	**41%**	28%	28%	28%
Parser line coverage	**55%**	41%	41%	41%
Parser branch coverage	**57%**	29%	29%	29%
Rules line coverage	**63%**	42%	42%	42%
Rules branch coverage	**71%**	24%	24%	24%
Parser class coverage	**88%** (22/25)	80% (20/25)		
Rules class coverage	**100%** (20/20)	90% (18/20)		

coverage—sometimes much higher coverage, as in the case of branch coverage for the rules components, where the corpus achieved 24% code coverage and the test suite achieved 71% code coverage. The last three columns show the results of an experiment in which we varied the size of the rule set. As can be seen from the fact that the coverage for the entire rule set, a partition of the rule set that only covered nominals, and a partition of the rule set that covered only verbs, are all equal, the number of rules processed was not a determiner of code coverage.

In a further experiment, we examined how code coverage is affected by variations in the size of the corpus. We monitored coverage as increasingly larger portions of the the corpus were processed. The results for line coverage are shown in Figure 1. (The results for branch coverage are very similar and are not shown.) The x axis shows the number of sentences processed. The thick solid line indicates line coverage for the entire application. The thin solid line indicates line coverage for the rules package. The broken line and the right y axis indicate the number of pattern matches.

As the figure shows quite clearly, increasing the size of the corpus does not lead to increasing code coverage. It is 39% when a single sentence has been processed, 40% when 51 sentences have been processed, and 41%—the highest value that it will reach—when 1,000 sentences have been processed. The coverage after processing 191,478 sentences—the entire corpus of almost 4,000,000 words—is no higher than it was at 1,000 sentences, and is barely higher than after processing a single sentence.

Thus, we see that the "naturally occurring data assumption" does not hold—from an engineering perspective, there is a clear advantage to using structured test suites.

This should not be taken as a claim that running an application against a large corpus is bad. In fact, we routinely do this, and have found bugs that were not uncovered in other ways. However, testing with a structured test suite should remain a primary element of natural language processing software testing.

It will be noted that even with the structured test suite, our code coverage was less than 60% overall, as predicted by Wieger's work, which shows that when software is developed without monitoring code coverage, typically only 50-60% of the code is executed by test suites [15] (p. 526). However, as soon as we tried to increase our code coverage, we almost immediately uncovered two "showstopper" bugs.

6   Discussion

Although our assay of the software testing status of biomedical natural language processing applications was crude, the findings are consistent with the claim that 7/20 biomedical natural language processing web sites have not been subjected to even the lowest, most superficial level of software testing. For the rest, we cannot conclude that they have been adequately tested—only that they appear to have benefited from at least the lowest, most superficial level of testing.

This absence of software testing and quality assurance comes despite the fact that like the mainstream NLP community, the biomedical natural language processing community has paid considerable attention to software *evaluation*. Some clarification of terminology is useful here. [10] distinguish between *gold-standard-based evaluation* and *feature-based evaluation*. This is completely analogous to the distinction between what we are referring to as evaluating software with respect to some metric (gold-standard-based evaluation) and what we are referring to as *testing* it, or attempting to find bugs (feature-based evaluation). The biomedical natural language processing community has participated enthusiastically in software evaluation via shared tasks—agreed-upon task definitions used to evaluate systems against a shared data set using centralized, third-party evaluation with a corpus (or a document collection) as input and with an agreed-upon implementation of a scoring metric. However, the community's investment in testing its products has apparently been much smaller. It has been suggested [20] that biomedical natural language processing applications are ready for use by working bioscientists. If this is the case, we argue that there is a moral obligation on the part of biomedical natural language processing practitioners to exercise due diligence and ensure that their applications do not just perform well against arbitrary metrics, but also behave as intended.

We showed in our experiments with building linguistically motivated test suites that such test suites, informed by the techniques of descriptive linguistics, are effective at granular characterization of performance across a wide variety of named entity recognition systems. We also demonstrated the surprising finding that such test suites could be used to predict global performance scores such as precision, recall, and F-measure (although only recall was predicted in our experiment) for specific equivalence classes (or, as linguists call them, natural classes) of inputs.

Drawing directly on a software engineering technique, we used a test suite to test the commonly held, if tacit, assumption that large corpora are the best testing material for natural language processing applications. We demonstrated that in fact even a small test suite can achieve much better code coverage than a very large corpus.

As a reviewer pointed out, most linguistic phenomena are Zipfian in nature. How far must we go in evaluating and handling the phenomena in the Zipfian tail? Steedman has an insightful observation on this question:

> We have come to believe that the linguists have forgotten Zipf's law, which says that most of the variance in linguistic behavior can be captured by a small part of the system.
>
> The linguists, on the other hand, think that it is we who have forgotten Zipf's law, which also says that most of the information about the language system as a whole is in the Long Tail.
>
> It is we who are at fault here, because the machine learning techniques that we rely on are actually very bad at inducing systems for which the crucial information is in rare events...
>
> One day. . . the Long Tail will come back to haunt us.

[21]

Even for work whose goal is not application-building but basic research, the costs of failing to attend to basic software testing and quality assurance issues can be quite severe. As Rob Knight has put it, "For scientific work, bugs don't just mean unhappy users who you'll never actually meet: they mean retracted publications and ended careers. It is critical that your code be fully tested before you draw conclusions from the results it produces." The recent case of Geoffrey Chang (see [16] for a succinct discussion) is illustrative. In 2006, he was a star of the protein crystallography world. That year he discovered a simple software error in his code which led to a reversal of the sign (positive versus negative) of two columns of numbers in his output. This led to a reversed prediction of handedness in the ABC transporter gene MsbA. This error had implications for the work of many other scientists in addition to his own. The story is an object lesson in the potential consequences of failure to attend to basic software testing and quality assurance issues, although his principled response to the situation suggests that in his case, those consequences will be limited to retracted publications and will not be career-ending (see [5] for the retractions). For the sorts of standard software testing techniques that we looked for in the work reported here, a considerable amount of good material is available, ranging from cookbook-like how-to manuals (e.g. [13]) to theoretical work [3,14,4]. Language processing presents a number of specific testing issues related to unique characteristics of the input data, and the literature on it is quite limited (but see [6,12,7] for some attempts to address this topic in the biomedical natural language processing domain, specifically). No non-trivial application is ever likely to be completely free of bugs, but that does not free us of the obligation to test for them. As we have shown here, approaches to doing so that are inspired by linguistic techniques are effective at granular characterization of performance, finding bugs, and achieving high code coverage.

Acknowledgements. We would like to thank our co-authors on some of the work cited in this paper. Lynette Hirschman (The MITRE Corporation) and Bob Carpenter (Alias-I) have discussed the general issues of software testing and quality assurance with us extensively. Martin Krallinger's web page at

biocreative.sourceforge.net

listing web-based biomedical NLP services was invaluable in performing the work reported here. Jonathan M. Cohen (Monterey County Public Defender's Office) and John Pestian (Cincinnati Children's Hospital Medical Center) helped us understand regulatory issues regarding medical software. This work was funded in part by grants NIH 5 R01 LM009254-06, NIH 5 R01 LM008111-07, NIH 5 R01 GM083649-04, and NIH 5 R01 LM009254-03 to Lawrence E. Hunter.

References

1. Baumgartner Jr., W.A., Lu, Z., Johnson, H.L., Gregory Caporaso, J., Paquette, J., Lindemann, A., White, E.K., Medvedeva, O., Bretonnel Cohen, K., Hunter, L.E.: Concept recognition for extraction protein interaction relations from biomedical text. Genome Biology 9(suppl. 2), S9 (2008)
2. Beizer, B.: Software testing techniques, 2nd edn. International Thomson Computer Press (1990)
3. Beizer, B.: Black-box testing: Techniques for functional testing of software and systems. Wiley (1995)
4. Binder, R.V.: Testing object-oriented systems: models, patterns, and tools. Addison-Wesley Professional (1999)
5. Chang, G., Roth, C.R., Reyes, C.L., Pornillos, O., Chen, Y.-J., Chen, A.P.: Letters: Retraction. Science 314, 1875 (2006)
6. Bretonnel Cohen, K., Tanabe, L., Kinoshita, S., Hunter, L.: A resource for constructing customized test suites for molecular biology entity identification systems. In: BioLINK 2004: Linking Biological Literature, Ontologies, and Databases: Tools for Users, pp. 1–8. Association for Computational Linguistics (2004)
7. Bretonnel Cohen, K., Baumgartner Jr., W.A., Hunter, L.: Software testing and the naturally occurring data assumption in natural language processing. In: Software Engineering, Testing, and Quality Assurance for Natural Language Processing, pp. 23–30. Association for Computational Linguistics (2008)
8. Food and Drug Administration, US Department of Health and Human Services, General principles of software validation: Final guidance for industry and FDA staff (2002)
9. Hakenberg, J., Leaman, R., Vo, N.H., Jonnalagadda, S., Sullivan, R., Miller, C., Tari, L., Baral, C., Gonzalez, G.: Efficient extraction of protein-protein interactions from full-text articles. IEEE/ACM Transactions on Computational Biology and Bioinformatics (July 2010)
10. Hirschman, L., Mani, I.: Evaluation. In: Mitkov, R. (ed.) The Oxford Handbook of Computational Linguistics, ch. 23. Oxford University Press (2003)
11. Hunter, L.E., Lu, Z., Firby, J., Baumgartner Jr., W.A., Johnson, H.L., Ogren, P.V., Bretonnel Cohen, K.: OpenDMAP: An open-source, ontology driven concept analysis engine, with applications to capturing knowledge regarding protein transport, protein interactions and cell-specific gene expression. BMC Bioinformatics 9(78) (2008)

12. Johnson, H.L., Bretonnel Cohen, K., Hunter, L.: A fault model for ontology mapping, alignment, and linking systems. In: Pacific Symposium on Biocomputing 2007, pp. 233–244. World Scientific Publishing (2007)
13. Kaner, C., Nguyen, H.Q., Falk, J.: Testing computer software, 2nd edn. John Wiley and Sons (1999)
14. Marick, B.: The craft of software testing: subsystem testing including object-based and object-oriented testing. Prentice Hall (1997)
15. McConnell, S.: Code complete, 2nd edn. Microsoft Press (2004)
16. Miller, G.: A scientist's nightmare: software problem leads to five retractions. Science 314, 1856–1857 (2006)
17. Oepen, S., Netter, K., Klein, J.: TSNLP – test suites for natural language processing. In: Nerbonne, J. (ed.) Linguistic Databases, ch. 2, pp. 13–36. CSLI Publications (1998)
18. Palmer, M., Finin, T.: Workshop on the evaluation of natural language processing systems. Computational Linguistics 16(3), 175–181 (1990)
19. Partee, B.H., ter Meulen, A., Wall, R.E.: Mathematical methods in linguistics. Springer (1990)
20. Rebholz-Schuhmann, D., Kirsch, H., Couto, F.: Facts from text—is text mining ready to deliver? PLoS Biology 3(2), 188–191 (2005)
21. Steedman, M.: On becoming a discipline. Computational Linguistics 34(1), 137–144 (2008)
22. Tanabe, L., John Wilbur, W.: Tagging gene and protein names in biomedical text. Bioinformatics 18(8), 1124–1132 (2002)
23. Tanabe, L., Xie, N., Thom, L.H., Matten, W., John Wilbur, W.: GENETAG: a tagged corpus for gene/protein name recognition. BMC Bioinformatics 6(suppl. 1), S4 (2005)
24. Verspoor, K., Bretonnel Cohen, K., Mani, I., Goertzel, B.: Introduction to BioNLP 2006. In: Linking Natural Language Processing and Biology: Towards Deeper Biological Literature Analysis, pp. iii–iv. Association for Computational Linguistics (2006)
25. Zweigenbaum, P., Demner-Fushman, D., Yu, H., Bretonnel Cohen, K.: Frontiers for biomedical text mining: current progress. Briefings in Bioinformatics 8(5) (2007)

Supporting Agile Software Development by Natural Language Processing

Barbara Plank[1], Thomas Sauer[2], and Ina Schaefer[3]

[1] University of Trento, Italy
[2] rjm business solutions GmbH, Lampertheim, Germany
[3] Technische Universität Braunschweig, Germany

Abstract. Agile software development puts more emphasis on working programs than on documentation. However, this may cause complications from the management perspective when an overview of the progress achieved within a project needs to be provided. In this paper, we outline the potential for applying natural language processing (NLP) in order to support agile development. We point out that using NLP, the artifacts created during agile software development activities can be traced back to the requirements expressed in user stories. This allows determining how far the project has progressed in terms of realized requirements.

Keywords: Agile Software Development, Project Management, Machine Learning, Natural Language Processing.

1 Introduction

Over the last decade, agile software development has evolved from a fiercely debated novelty into standard practice of many organizations. When properly applied, agile software development methodologies such as Scrum [14] help to develop software more predictably, more reliably, and with higher overall quality. This is mainly achieved by a iterative, incremental approach: the development process is split into iterations, which in Scrum are also known as *sprints*. In each sprint, a working increment of the system is realized. The development activities to do so are split into manageable chunks of work, so-called tasks. Developers are kept motivated by avoiding excessive documentation and unnecessary tools or procedures. An overview of agile software development using Scrum is given in Figure 1.

In Scrum, requirements are expressed as *user stories*, which describe a certain system feature from the perspective of a stakeholder [4]. User stories can refer to all sorts of requirements, including functional as well as non-functional system properties. When starting a new sprint, i.e., a new development cycle, the development team chooses as many user stories as they believe can be turned into a working increment of the product.

The *product owner* is responsible for providing enough user stories such that a working increment of the product can be actually implemented during an iteration. That is, before a new sprint can start, the product owner needs to

A. Moschitti and B. Plank (Eds.): EternalS 2013, CCIS 379, pp. 91–102, 2013.

have the user stories readily identified that are most important at the current stage of the development. After the sprint is done, the product owner is also responsible for deciding whether a user story has been sufficiently realized, or whether there is work remaining.

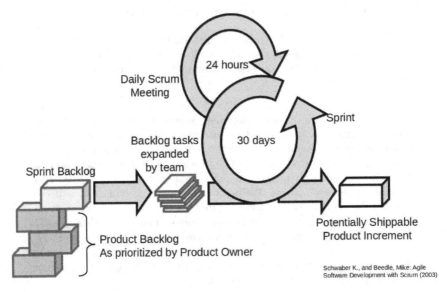

Fig. 1. Agile Development with Scrum

This requires that the product owner has a deep understanding of what the team has actually produced during the sprint. Especially when the product owner has to fulfill other duties in the organization, it can be overwhelmingly complex and time-consuming to keep up with the current status of the development. During a sprint, developers typically coordinate themselves in daily Scrum meetings, personal communication, etc., but the product owner is usually only a passive participant. For agile software development by Scrum to work, however, it is crucial that the product owner has the relevant requirements and user stories for the system to be developed and their priorities available when needed. Clearly, the product owner is not omniscient and may sometimes not be aware of recent development activities. Therefore, a monitoring process that can help the product owner to take decisions can prevent taking wrong priorities and thus a waste of resources.

In this position paper, we propose the use of natural language processing (NLP) techniques to overcome the problem that the product owner needs to keep track of the current status of development and the completed or non-completed user stories. By analyzing the artifacts created by the developers, such as source code, code comments or bug reports, connections can be established between the user stories that are planned to be completed during the sprint and the actual progress achieved by the development team. As the artifacts that are produced usually are not captured by some formal representation, natural language processing techniques are promising in order to automatically discover these connections. We propose a two step approach: in the first phase, *linking*, connections between artifacts and agile practices (user stories) need to be established; we can here build on prior work on traceability between software artifacts, e.g. [3,9] and initial work on linking user stories to lines of code [12], to be further discussed in Section 4. In the second phase, *information aggregation*, the previously connected data will be used for information aggregation. The goal is to abstract from the single information items found and advance current technologies in order to support the project owner by automatically providing information on the progress status to support agile project management decisions.

This paper is structured as follows: In Section 2, we review the background on development artifacts produced in Scrum and on natural language processing. In Section 3, we describe our approach. In Section 4, we discuss related work. In Section 5, we summarize this paper with an outlook to future work.

2   Background

User stories in Scrum often follow a certain template to express the roles involved, the goals to achieve, and the business value connected with the requirement. For instance, [4] suggests to express user stories in the format:

"As a (role) I want (some goal) so that (benefit)"

Figure 2 shows an example user story for implementing a string processing method. When starting a new sprint, the development team splits each user story into smaller tasks that can be accomplished in a single day. Typical tasks include implementation activities, writing unit tests, or reviewing code. For the example, there could be two tasks: the first task includes the implementation of the fancy case method and the second task concerns testing the implemented method.

> User Story 101:.
> As a string manipulation library user, I want to have a
> fancy case method in order to gain fancy cased strings.
> - The fancy case method should print the characters of a
> string alternating in upper and lower case.
> - Whitespace should be ignored.

Fig. 2. Example of a user story for string manipulation taken from [8]

Many development teams prefer to store the user stories and tasks for a sprint using physical task boards, index cards etc. But, there are numerous project management applications that allow keeping track of the user stories, tasks and their allocation to the different team members. For our approach, we assume that at least the product owner uses an electronic backlog to keep track of the user stories.

2.1   Development Artifacts

During a sprint, developers typically use a large variety of tools for their development activities, including IDEs, code repositories, bug tracking systems, etc. This leads to a large number of artifacts that are created besides the actual implementation when the Sprint team works on their tasks. Some of them follow some formal representation including a well-defined structure while others are more ad-hoc and mainly consist of natural language text without an external structure. The artifacts that we consider in our approach are the following. They are listed approximately in the following order: from more to less structured information (e.g. from code comments to instant messages) and according to the closeness to the source code. Some example artifacts for our running example are given in Figure 3.

> Code comments:
> `// fancy case method, alternated casing`
>
> Unit test methods:
> `testFancyCaseMethod()`
>
> Commit messages:
> `commit #123: implemented user story 101`
> `...`
> `commit #145: fixed bug in fancycase method`

Fig. 3. Example Artifacts for the user story given in Figure 2

Code Comments: In order to obtain code that is easy to debug and to maintain, code comments should be introduced at the relevant places to document the functionality of single methods or classes. For instance, using JavaDoc, these comments are placed within the actual code using special annotations from which an external documentation can be generated. Also unfinished issues in the code can be marked with ToDo such that these remaining issues can be tracked by the IDE. Both code comments and todo entries are natural text which can refer to tasks or to user stories.

Unit Test Definitions: Along the lines of test-driven development [2], the tests are written together with the implementation or even before the actual implementation. The tests refer to methods or classes in the implementation and may contain comments in natural language as well which state which scenarios from user stories are tested with the defined test cases. In the Java world, these test definitions are usually written using JUnit[1] such that they can conveniently be executed from the IDE.

Commit Messages: When a versioning system, such as Subversion or Git, is used, each developer adds the code he has implemented to complete a task or a smaller chunk of work, into a central repository. Each commit is usually accompanied

---

[1] `http://junit.sourceforge.net`

with a *commit message* which is usually natural language text stating which changes or additions have been made. The commit message may for instance refer to the addressed task.

Bug Reports: Deficiencies found while testing or reviewing the implementation are usually stored in a bug tracking system, such as Bugzilla[2]. Each issue found is commonly described with a unique identifier and a detailed description when and how the software misbehaves. When the problem is fixed, this is also entered into the bug tracking system, e.g., with a reference to the corresponding commit in the versioning system.

Build Scripts and Reports: Continuous integration systems such as Hudson[3] are often used to automatically integrate and compile the different components of a software system. Further, automatic testing can be triggered. In combination with the results reported, the integration steps currently configured can provide insight about the status the project is in and which parts are already finished.

Task Lists: In order to keep track of the tasks and their allocation to different team members, project management tools such as TinyPM[4] are typically used. Furthermore, the status of each task is maintained, e.g., whether a task is still pending, has been already started, or is already completed. Tasks can also be associated to the user stories within such a system. Thus, a project management system can provide the most detailed input from the management perspective, assuming that the team members keep the status of the tasks up-to-date. This facts needs to be validated from the other artifacts that are created during development.

Wiki Pages: Many organizations use Wiki systems to manage the knowledge obtained while working on a project. This may include best practices, lessons learned or specific design decisions. Wiki pages usually consist of natural language text that is only weakly structured by, e.g., marking section headings.

Calendar Entries: Group calendars are ubiquitous tools for most development teams. They may store information about meetings concerning specific issues within the development, such as decisions how to solve specific tasks. The information about the date and time of the meeting and its content, and maybe also the according meeting minutes, can provide insights into the progress of the project.

IM messages and social network postings: Instant messaging and social networks can be used by developers for quick communication with colleagues about specific issues during development, e.g., if a framework or API does not work as expected. These messages and posting may refer to tasks or the outcome of tasks and, thus, may be valuable in determining progress.

---

[2] http://www.bugzilla.org
[3] http://www.hudson-ci.org
[4] http://www.tinypm.com

This is by far not an exhaustive list, but it shows the possible artifacts that can we exploited for the proposed approach. As we have seen, the artifacts contain various levels of textual information (from short descriptions to entire Wiki pages), thereby presenting an interesting challenge for NLP, which we will introduce next.

2.2 Natural Language Processing

Natural Language Processing (NLP) [7] is an interdisciplinary field between computer science, artificial intelligence, machine learning and linguistics concerned with the study of computational approaches to understand and/or produce human (natural) language. Building systems that are able to do so is a difficult task, given the intrinsic properties of natural language. One of the major challenges for NLP is the *ambiguity* of language, exemplified in the following sentence: *The product owner gave her user stories.* Humans usually have no trouble identifying the intended meaning (that the product owner gave some user stories to 'her', presumably a software developer), while a computer usually identifies many possible readings. For example, an alternative reading is that the product owner gives some kind of stories to 'her user', thus identifying 'her' as possessive pronoun and splitting the compound noun 'user story'. Ambiguity is pertaining to all levels of linguistic processing. For instance, structural ambiguity (whether 'her' attaches to the verb or noun) or word-level ambiguity (whether her is a personal or a possessive pronoun).

While early approaches to NLP were mainly symbolic and rule-based, the field has changed dramatically since the development of annotated corpora (text collections), the introduction of machine learning and the associated growth and availability of computational power, leading to data-driven statistical approaches for learning. Current research largely focuses on the use of data-driven approaches to learn from annotated (supervised learning), partially labeled data (semi-supervised) or unlabeled data (unsupervised learning/clustering).

Some of the NLP tasks include, amongst others: part-of-speech (POS) tagging (determining the part of speech, or word-class, for each word in a sentence), named entity recognition (NER, given a text, determine which items in the text refer to, e.g. proper names, locations, geopolitical entities), parsing (extracting the syntactic structure of natural language sentences), relation extraction (RE, identify relationships between entities in text, e.g. who is working for whom), semantic role labeling (SRL, sometimes also called shallow semantic parsing, the detection of the semantic arguments associated with the predicate or verb of a sentence and their classification into their specific roles, e.g. agent, patient), Machine Translation (automatic translation between texts in different languages) and sentiment analysis (also known as opinion mining; extracting subjective information from text, e.g. opinion statements, overall polarity).

We here propose to use NLP to analyze the natural language-based artifacts created during the software development process. For instance, natural language parsing is the task of uncovering the syntactic structure of natural language sentences, which is represented in forms of trees. For example, if we apply a constituent parser (a parser that provides a hierarchical structure in which smaller parts are combined into larger parts called phrases, e.g. a *noun phrase* denoted NP) to the user story shown in Figure 2, we obtain the syntactic parse tree shown in Figure 4.

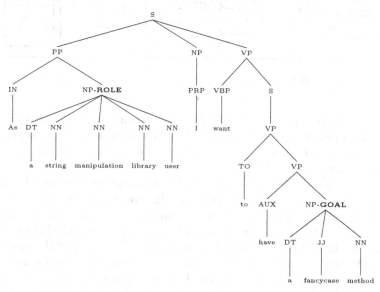

Fig. 4. A syntactic parse tree for the sentence "As a string manipulation library user, I want to have a fancycase method" from the example user story (punctuation omitted, abbreviated for space reasons). The tree is enriched with the target entity information (in bold face).

The same process can be applied to the artifacts: parsing the commit messages, the code comments, etc. Based on the syntactic structure, a classifier can be trained that determines the constituents that encode **ROLE**, **GOAL** or **BENEFIT** of a user story (indicated in bold face in Figure 4) and similarly of the artifacts. This leads to a possible structured instance representation that can be exploited, as discussed in the next section.

3   Approach

In order to establish a connection between the user stories on one side and the artifacts on the other site, we need a mechanism to associate them based on their similarity. In this section, we outline our proposed approach to apply NLP to artifacts obtained during agile software development in order to support the product owner's decisions.

To this end, we propose a two-step approach as depicted in Figure 5: In the first *linking* step, we establish connections between user stories and the development artifacts (cf. Section 2.1). In the second *information aggregation*

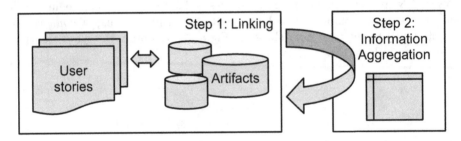

Fig. 5. Overview of the proposed approach

step, we classify user stories according to their status (to be implemented/not yet started, in progress, completed) based on the artifacts found. This helps the product owner to get a better understanding of the current status of the project at the user story level.

In the first linking step (cf. Figure 6), the information contained in the development artifacts is analyzed in order to discover which artifacts belong to the realization of which user story. For instance, a code comment or a commit message can refer to the implementation of the fancy case method of the example user story in Figure 2 allowing to link it to the first task of the user story. Additionally, the comments of a JUnit test can reference parts of the user story such that the test case can be associated to the second task of this user story. The artifacts that have tight links to the code, such as code comments or commit messages, can be augmented with information derived from bug reports or development Wiki. Also other sources of information might be exploited (which are less structured and more distant to the code, as shown in Figure 6), such as instant messaging (IM) within the company network or social network posts.

To make the linking step technically more concrete from the NLP perspective, we need to reason about i) possible instance representations of the artifacts and the user stories, and ii) possible learning mechanisms able to identify similar objects.

For the instance representation, a first attempt might consist in applying information retrieval [10] techniques: representing the information contained in the artifact or user story in a simple *bag-of-words* model in the *vector space* (i.e. counting how often a word appeared in a user story, possibly weighted). If we also want to link actual source code to user stories, then it will be also necessary to identify and split source code identifiers into actual words [9]. Then, similarity between these unstructured objects (vectors) can be calculated based on the angle between the feature vectors in the vector space (e.g. their *cosine similarity*). Alternatively, deep natural language processing might be applied to gather structured objects. For instance, the example user story could be represent as shown in Figure 7, where natural language parsing and argument classification has been applied. This representation could be further enriched with other NLP tools like a semantic role labeler, a named entity recognizer, or distributional semantic techniques. Then, machine learning algorithms able to deal with

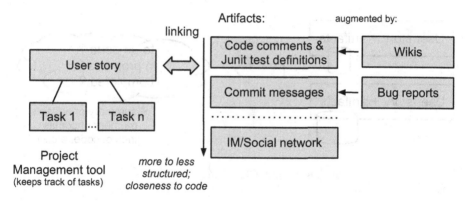

Fig. 6. Step 1: Linking User Stories with Artifacts

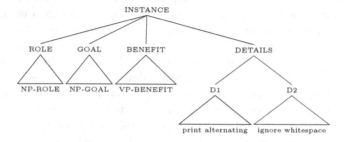

Fig. 7. Possible instance representation. The roof is a compact representation to represent tree information.

structured input data, like tree-kernel based support vector machines [5,11] could be applied to learn a similarity function in the structured space.

Once a mapping between artifacts and user stories has been established, the second information aggregation step is performed (cf. Figure 8): a classifier is trained to determine the status of the user story: "to be implemented/not yet started", "in progress", "completed". The amount of artifacts found in the first stage, as well as related meta-data (e.g. number of lines of code associated with a commit message, amount of JUnit tests related to the user story, status of unit tests, number of bugs fixed, etc.) could be exploited to train a system to classify user stories into the three categories, while further giving aggregated information on the collected artifacts. For instance, if in the example user story (cf. Figure 2), code comments and commit messages referring to the first task of implementing the fancy case method are found the user story is classified as "in progress". If also test cases are found with a positive reporting and no bug reports referring to the fancy case method are found, the user story can be labeled as "completed".

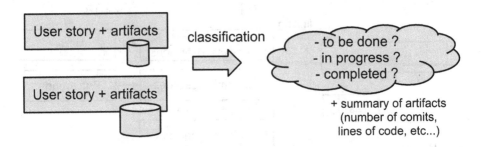

Fig. 8. Step 2: Classifying User Stories

4 Related Work

Monitoring development activities for supporting project management has been discussed before as *software project telemetry* [6]. The development environment is instrumented by software "sensors" attached to editors, test suites or bug-tracking databases. The sensors continuously send data to a central analysis component, where metrics of interest such as code churn or build failures are calculated. This enables detecting unwanted development in time. In contrast to our approach, management roles such as product owners have to draw their own conclusions how current activities are connected to specific requirements.

Connecting user stories with concrete agile development activities is discussed in [12]. The authors present a tool for associating newly created or recently modified lines of code with the individual tasks of a user story. While the initial association has to be made manually, subsequent development activity is automatically tracked by analyzing revision control usage. However, links between user stories and higher-level development artifacts other than source code are not supported.

For reducing the efforts required to link requirements with development results, *automated traceability* [3] has been suggested. By applying information retrieval algorithms, the likelihood of connections between specific requirements and code documents, UML diagrams, etc. is determined by, e.g., calculating the similarity of terms. A survey of applicable techniques can be found in [15]. The NLP approach presented in this paper augments these techniques by specifically supporting the concept of user stories in agile software development. If we also include actual source code, then an important preprocessing step related to this is the work on automatically splitting source code identifiers into component terms (e.g. *drawRectangle* or *drawrect* into *draw* and *rectangle*), as done in [9].

NLP has been already found useful for supporting specific agile techniques, such as behavior driven development [8]. Here, product owners provide an abstract test script for each user story. Using an ontology, these scripts are related with their corresponding implementation. When the development team is working on a new user story and its test script, NLP techniques are applied for extracting the nouns and verbs contained in the story. The extracted entities enable to find similar test steps by consulting the ontology, fostering efficient test code reuse.

5   Conclusion and Future Work

In this paper, we have presented the idea of using natural language processing techniques for supporting agile development. By analyzing the artifacts created during development activities, such as writing code, committing a patch, or filing a bug report, connections are established between the user stories which represent the system requirements. This supports the roles representing the stakeholders, such as product owners in a Scrum project, to understand what the team has actually produced during a development cycle.

Although user stories are expressed in free-form text, they are typically not free of form. Instead, certain templates are followed, which encode roles, goals or organizational benefits. Similar applies to artifacts such as source code, commit messages, or bug reports. This allows using proven NLP techniques to create structured representations, which in turn enables finding interdependencies.

The next step and challenge is to create a suitable training set to evaluate the presented approach. For example, an agile open source software project can be taken as a starting point.

Acknowledgements. This research has been supported by the European Communitys Seventh Framework Programme (FP7/2007-2013) under the grants #247758 (EternalS) and #288024 (LiMoSINe).

References

1. Ambriola, V., Gervasi, V.: On the systematic analysis of natural language requirements with circe. Autom. Softw. Eng. 13(1), 107–167 (2006)
2. Beck, K.: Test Driven Development By Example. Addison-Wesley (2002)
3. Cleland-Huang, J., Settimi, R., Romanova, E.: Best practices for automated traceability. Computer 40(6), 27–35 (2007)
4. Cohn, M.: User Stories Applied for Agile Software Development. Addison-Wesley (2004)
5. Collins, M., Duffy, N.: Convolution kernels for natural language. In: Proceedings of NIPS (2001)
6. Johnson, P.M., Kou, H., Paulding, M., Zhang, Q., Kagawa, A., Yamashita, T.: Improving software development management through software project telemetry. IEEE Software 22(4), 76–85 (2005)
7. Jurafsky, D., Martin, J.H.: Speech and Language Processing. Prentice Hall Series in Artificial Intelligence. Prentice Hall (2008)
8. Landhäußer, M., Genaid, A.: Connecting user stories and code for test development. In: Proc. of the 3rd International Workshop on Recommendation Systems for Software Engineering (RSSE 2012), pp. 33–37 (2012)

9. Madani, N., Guerrouj, L., Di Penta, M., Gueheneuc, Y., Antoniol, G.: Recognizing words from source code identifiers using speech recognition techniques. In: 2010 14th European Conference on Software Maintenance and Reengineering (CSMR), pp. 68–77 (March 2010)
10. Manning, C., Raghavan, P., Schütze, H.: Introduction to information retrieval. Cambridge University Press (2008)
11. Moschitti, A.: A study on convolution kernels for shallow semantic parsing. In: Proceedings of the 42nd Meeting of the ACL, Barcelona, Spain (2004)
12. Ratanotayanon, S., Sim, S.E., Gallardo-Valencia, R.: Supporting program comprehension in agile with links to user stories. In: AGILE Conference, pp. 26–32. IEEE Computer Society (2009)
13. Sawyer, P., Rayson, P., Garside, R.: Revere: Support for requirements synthesis from documents. Information Systems Frontiers 4(3), 343–353 (2002)
14. Schwaber, K., Beedle, M.: Agile Software Development with Scrum. Prentice Hall (2001)
15. Winkler, S., von Pilgrim, J.: A survey of traceability in requirements engineering and model-driven development. Software and Systems Modeling 9, 529–565 (2010)

Anomaly Detection in the Cloud: Detecting Security Incidents via Machine Learning*

Matthias Gander[1], Michael Felderer[1], Basel Katt[1], Adrian Tolbaru[1], Ruth Breu[1], and Alessandro Moschitti[2]

[1] Institute of Computer Science, University of Innsbruck, Austria
[2] Information Engineering and Computer Science Department, University of Trento, Italy

Abstract. Cloud computing is now on the verge of being embraced as a serious usage-model. However, while outsourcing services and workflows into the cloud provides indisputable benefits in terms of flexibility of costs and scalability, there is little advance in security (which can influence reliability), transparency and incident handling. The problem of applying the existing security tools in the cloud is twofold. First, these tools do not consider the specific attacks and challenges of cloud environments, e.g., cross-VM side-channel attacks. Second, these tools focus on attacks and threats at only one layer of abstraction, e.g., the network, the service, or the workflow layers. Thus, the semantic gap between events and alerts at different layers is still an open issue. The aim of this paper is to present ongoing work towards a Monitoring-as-a-Service anomaly detection framework in a hybrid or public cloud. The goal of our framework is twofold. First it closes the gap between incidents at different layers of cloud-sourced workflows, namely we focus both on the workflow and the infrastructure layers. Second, our framework tackles challenges stemming from cloud usage, like multi-tenancy. Our framework uses complex event processing rules and machine learning, to detect populate user-specified metrics that can be used to assess the security status of the monitored system.

Keywords: Monitoring, Behaviour, Anomaly Detection, Clustering, Fingerprints.

1 Introduction

Building your own monolithic IT infrastructure is slowly rendered obsolete by cost efficient cloud solutions that promise on-demand scalability with leased

* This work is supported by QE LaB-Living Models for Open Systems (FFG 822740), and SECTISSIMO (FWF 20388) and has been partially supported by the European Community's Seventh Framework Programme (FP7/2007-2013) under the grants #247758: ETERNALS – Trustworthy Eternal Systems via Evolving Software, Data and Knowledge, and #288024: LiMoSINE – Linguistically Motivated Semantic aggregation engiNes.

A. Moschitti and B. Plank (Eds.): EternalS 2013, CCIS 379, pp. 103–116, 2013.
© Springer-Verlag Berlin Heidelberg 2013

hardware, i.e. by contracting Infrastructure as a Service (IaaS) provider such as Amazon's "elastic compute cloud" EC2 cloud) [1, 2]. Therefore it is not surprising that corporations opt to outsource IT related computing units, such as hosts or services, to such clouds (*cloud-sourcing*) to become cloud *tenants*. Leading analysts forecast a dramatic increase of cloud services revenue, i.e. Gartner, Inc. forecast Software as a Service (SaaS) to increase 17.9% from the 2011 revenue of $12.3 billion.[1] Cloud tenants though, often have to pay a price. Increased scalability of resources demands dynamical compositions of computing machinery resulting in design inherent weaknesses, for instance, tenants share the same cloud and are potentially allowed to interact by design [3].

This results in potentially hostile machines residing within the corporate network that has to be secured. Hostile machines on the network tear security holes in multiple layers of computation. Infrastructure items, such as hosts, can be broken into by a competing company to attain confidential information about its users and other data that is stored on the machine. This in turn allows workflows to be changed, i.e. by breaking in a system and patching the codebase or the platform itself [4, 5], or simply by reverse engineering workflows and creating rogue clients. A thusly changed workflow has semantical consequences on its logic, for instance, bypassed checks for sufficient funds in a credit card application, a compromised XACML (or Kerberos) infrastructure that grants authorizational access to restricted entities.

Another problem is that attacks themselves have become sneakier. Attackers tend to use more advanced techniques, and more persistence to eventually mask an attack as inside job[2]. For example, if credentials of legitimate service users are stolen and information is leaked gradually and persistently over a longer time period. Such attacks usually manifest in a change of behavior of entities involved in any given activity (e.g. behavioural changes observed in off-key working hours, spiking access over document data etc.).

To decrease the chance of successful attacks, security monitoring was introduced to analyse events committed by sensors in the corporate network. The analysis of events usually involves *signature-based* methods. Features, extracted from logged event data, are compared to features in attack signatures which in turn are provided by experts [6, 7]. Other approaches, e.g. *anomaly detection*, often make use of machine learning-based algorithms [8]. Anomalies are an unexpected event (or a series of unexpected events) that exhibit a significant change in behaviour of an entity, for example, a user. If anomalous behavior can be distinguished from normal behavior by hard bounds that are known beforehand, then signature-based approaches can be used to classify attacks immediately. However, when it is hard to specify all entities and their normal behaviour completely beforehand, then statistical measures have to be used to classify deviations in oder to detect possible attacks.

---

[1] http://www.gartner.com/it/page.jsp?id=1963815, Accessed: July 30, 2012.
[2] http://www.schneier.com/blog/archives/2011/11/advanced_persis.html, Accessed: July 30, 2012.

Unfortunately, probabilities and patterns of unwanted behaviour are very hard to procure and labeled training data for a new system is sparse [8, 9]. But it is reasonable to assume that most activity in a network is not triggered by compromised machines and attacks are represented by only a tiny fraction of the overall behaviour. Therefore, methods provided by unsupervised learning yield outliers, which in turn may represent attacks [9–11]. Unsupervised learning can roughly be classified in, nearest-neighbour, rule-mining, statistical, and clustering techniques. Each of which have advantages and disadvantages, depending on how they are used, see Chandola et al. [11]. For our purpose of grouping anomalous instances, clustering seems best suited. The disadvantages of clustering, i.e. the complexity of clustering algorithms and possible misclassifications, can be reduced by leveraging optimized algorithms, assumptions, and false-positive reductions [9, 12].

Both methods, signature-based and anomaly-based, have strengths and weaknesses. The main drawback of signature-based methods is the inherent limitation that they always have to consult the signature database to match detected features with the information therein [9]. If a new attack is out, it is probable that the signature database does not contain the latest attack pattern. Anomaly-based detection techniques, on other hand, have their true potential in detecting previously unseen patterns [8]. A common limitation both detection techniques share is a lack of "context". This context needs to provide information about inherent relations among users, services they use, the hosts from which they operate, and for which workflow they are assigned to. For instance, it is not sufficient to know that a service has longer than average response time, the correlation of response time and measurable changes of user and network host behaviour offers more valuable clues.

In order to get benefits from signature- and anomaly-based monitoring we propose to combine them into a context-based anomaly detection framework. This framework consists of three main tiers:

i The specification of a DSL which allows to model the cloud-sourced IT landscape in detail such that workflows can be specified, monitoring rules can be generated, and computing entities can be put into relation.
ii The detection of workflow aberrations, or semantic gaps, caused by attacks via Complex Event Processing (CEP) based on monitoring rules generated by the model. CEP is a signature-based method to analyze event streams in a midtoupper size IT infrastructure [13]. The purpose of CEP is to derive more meaningful events (in this case alerts).
iii The detection of abnormal entities, i.e. users, services, network hosts, and workflows, by leveraging unsupervised machine learning, to detect unforeseen changes in the behavior.

The application of our framework in a cloud-sourced health-care environment provides the means necessary to unravel the following incidents:

– *Semantic Gaps.* A document retrieval workflow doctor accessing the database without proof of first having received a permission token, replay attacks, workflow aberrations through patched code.

- *Anomalies.* An increase of service activity, service calls at unusual hours, abnormal users, detectable by a gradually increasing number of document requests, suspiciously active hosts, but also a change in flow behavior of service calls and network hosts (i.e. payload analysis of web-service parameters). The entities, services, users, hosts, workflows, constituting the unusual behaviour are labeled as anomaly.

The paper will continue with a description of the framework in Section 2, including the DSL 2.1, the usage of CEP 2.2, profiling entities 2.3 and anomaly detection via fingerprints 2.4. Section 3 depicts the used architecture and Sections 5 and 4 discuss future work and related work respectively.

2   Framework Overview

In this section we discuss the framework in more detail. We begin with the DSL to specify the IT infrastructure consisting of workflows, services, hosts, users, and their relations. This in turn leads to the discussion of how CEP is included in the framework. Afterwards our discussion will continue with details about the profiling of entities for anomaly detection purposes, i.e. discuss the different profiles, the features for fingerprints, the clustering method and distance measure, and round it up with a description of the architecture.

Every monitoring system needs events to determine the actual state of the system. Our framework expects events from the infrastructure, in form of TCP and UDP packets sent from the machines in the network, and in form of service calls. TCP and UDP packets are aggregated as flows that have multiple characteristics, such as, source, destination, ports, time, among others, duration. Service events are used to derive the current state of the services, show user behaviour (i.e. access requests), and give general information on the state of workflows. Information that should be present is, the duration of a call, the time, the user, and the object id that was requested.

2.1   A DSL for IT Landscapes

The use of metamodels or domain specific languages (DSL) is not uncommon [14, 15], their main use is to provide the vocabulary for experts to let them express their knowledge to represent the system in a textual [3] (or graphical) model. These models can later be accessed for look-ups, reasoning, and/or code generation.

Our DSL, therefore, allows the creation of a model that in turn allows harvesting information of entities (i.e. traceability of deployed entities to model information) and monitoring rule-generation. The model in Figure 1 reuses concepts from Breu et al. [14, 15], for example the introduction of multiple conceptual layers. The event-driven process chain paradigm [16] that is used in the model facilitates the modeling process, since it allows to represent services through

---

[3] xText: http://www.eclipse.org/Xtext, Accessed: July 20, 2012.

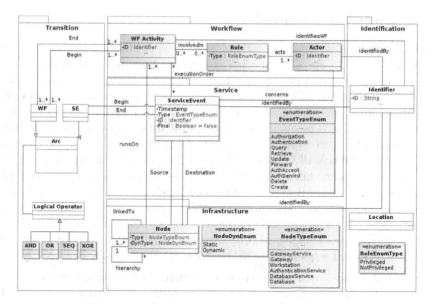

Fig. 1. A language to describe an IT landscape

their behaviour in form of events. A workflow activity, therefore, is not modeled via services and their call-sequence but rather as a series of events.

A model derived from the DSL contains three layers, *Workflow, Service* and *Infrastructure.* The workflow layer contains three classes, these are *WF Activity, Role,* and *Actor.* Activities and service events are related by arcs (*Arc*) which describe the way a workflow is executed. These arcs can have different types, i.e. *AND, OR, XOR, SEQ.* SEQ denotes that if said arc lies between two workflow activities A and B, then A is followed by B. *AND, OR* and *XOR* relate events in a boolean fashion. For instance A AND B,C denotes that after A, B and C is executed. Roles, *role* is a set of responsibilities and obligations for a stakeholder, that can influence heuristics during the analysis of events. As discussed above, services are not modeled directly, but are modelled as *ServiceEvent* of various types (*EventTypeEnum*). Event emitters are services, on top of hosts. Hence, among other features provided by the service event, i.e. variable ones such as timestamps and session ids (to identify the *Actor*), we assume a source and a destination pointing to the hosts that were responsible for the event. This allows us to connect the service layer to the infrastructure layer. Hosts (Node in the model) can be of various types (*NodeType*), this makes it easier to map events to their corresponding workflow activity during runtime.

Identifier defines the set of identifiers, i.e. all elements are connected to it via *identifiedBy,* such as hosts, service events, and actors are identified by it (via UUID and a location). The elements doing the execution are hosts from the infrastructure, hence the (*runsOn*) class.

2.2 Complex Event Processing

To monitor proper execution of systems, rule-based approaches tend to be used, i.e. in form of CEP. For CEP much research has been invested in query languages to handle the stream of events in query-based languages similar to SQL[4], ESPER[5], Oracle CEP[6], Coral8[7] and Aleri[8]. In our case we need to listen for events that are modelled beforehand, i.e. we need to listen for sequences that represent a workflow. These sequences give all the information necessary to infer who is responsible for certain actions. Part of our work focuses on the creation of CEP rules automatically based on the model created by the expert. For CEP rules the Esper Query Language (EQL)[9] in combination with the Esper CEP engine was chosen, since it is open source (GPL GNU Public License v2.0), has an active community and has shown potential in several benchmarks [17]. The translation from workflow models to query rules is straight forward, since EQL provides the same boolean logical connectives as our model and also provides the possibility to model sequences $\xrightarrow[seq]{}$. For instance, the formula $Ev_0 \xrightarrow[seq]{} Ev_1$ is only satisfied if and only if Ev_0 is emmitted before Ev_1. In summary a workflow model, as used for compliance detection, is nothing more than a series of CEP rules that are verified by the CEP engine.

2.3 Profiling of Entities

To determine anomalies in the activity of a corporate network, the accounting information of banks, or more general in usage behaviours, it is common to first create a profile that describes a normal behaviour of key entities [18, 19]. The profile types, *service, user, host,* and *workflow,* that we consider reflect the key entities that are involved in an on-line data processing. Gartner, Inc. [20] states, for instance, that there is the need for *user profiling* to monitor user behaviour to prevent data theft. *Service profiles* are needed to determine, among others, a gradual decrease of performance compared to itself or an overall different behaviour from other services. Communication patterns among hosts also need to be considered in form of a *host profile.* Outliers in each of these types of entities have an impact on the performance/security of *workflows* and their activity profile.

Assume, for instance, a compromised machine that gradually increases the number of requests for classified object information in the name of an existing user U over service S by using machines $M_{0..n}$. Normally, this is not easy to trace, especially if U has permissions to query restricted information (no CEP alerts will be generated). A time-based analysis, though, yields detectable changes

---

[4] http://www.w3schools.com/sql/default.asp, Accessed: July 20, 2012.
[5] http://esper.codehaus.org/, Accessed: July 20, 2012.
[6] http://tinyurl.com/OracleCEP, Accessed: July 20, 2012.
[7] http://tinyurl.com/Coral8CEP, Accessed: July 20, 2012.
[8] http://tinyurl.com/AleriStreaming, Accessed: July 20, 201.2.
[9] http://esper.codehaus.org/, Accessed: July 20, 2012.

in the behaviour of U, S, and $M_{0..n}$. These are, more queries in U's name, more queries spread to machines $M_{0..n}$, more queries at unusual hours for S by U, and at the end, a detectable change of the workflow behaviour itself. The profiles are further refined into, an *immediate, hourly,* and *monthly* track.

   i To perform an on-line analysis of individual service events, CEP is used. CEP alerts have an immediate impact on the immediate track as well as statistical information gathered from the event itself, i.e. z-scores from parameters, duration, and the payload.

  ii An hourly track allows to aggregate some more information about hourly deviances, for instance, the average number of calls for a service, the number of its users, average call duration, extreme values such as maximum duration and minimum duration, the number of alerts produced by the immediate track during selected hours, and more.

 iii To assess more subtle patterns of deviance, a longer time-period is needed. To give an example consider the following scenario of a persistent attack. A competing company or government managed to break into the system and hides its activities of espionage, e.g., by leaking of sensitive documents, in form of an insider attack. For this, the real attackers stole the credentials of some user U to gradually query more and more documents, for instance creating 2-3% more queries per day (hour) than was normal. The immediate and hourly track are not built to detect such subtle aberrations and, hence, fail to detect them. The comparison of absolute access numbers over, for instance a monthly basis, shows a huge increase of query activity.

Information from the hourly (h) and monthly (m) track of an entity is represented by fingerprints (F_h^e, F_m^e) and represent, hence, a measure of the overall behaviour of the selected entity (e). Fingerprints are basically feature vectors $\mathbf{v}_i = (v_{i0}, \ldots, v_{in-1})$, containing continuous data. Fingerprints contain for instance, the number of CEP alerts in an hour, the number of alerts raised from immediate profiles, or z-score outliers. Our framework uses these fingerprints to compare its behaviour to other entities' behaviours but also to measure potential deviances of its own behaviour over time.

2.4   Clustering Fingerprints for Anomaly Detection

To determine abnormal entities in relation to other entities of the same type it is necessary to compare individual features of a profile and attain a sense of distance. Since individual characteristics of a profile might not change sufficiently to determine that an entity is an anomaly, we take into consideration all of the individual features that were collected. To take all features into consideration clustering can be used [21]. Clustering makes use of the inherent structure of data and groups data instances (clustering) by common attributes and a similarity measure. After the outliers have been found, the model can then be used to further link entities and detect correlations among outlying users, and, for instance, services. Figure 2 summarizes how the layers are related.

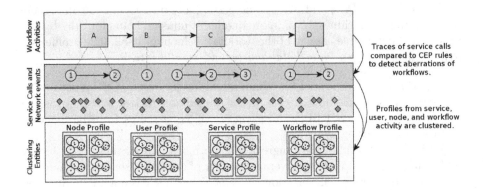

Fig. 2. Overview of connecting the layers

Although other distance measures exist, e.g., Jaccard, Dice, and Russell/Rao [21, 22], which have their use when comparing dichotomous data, the measure of distance which we use is the Euclidean metric, see Formula 1. It gives us the opportunity to measure distances of continuous multi-dimensional variables, i.e., $\mathbf{v}_i \in R^d$.

$$d(\mathbf{v}_i, \mathbf{v}'_i) = \left(\sum_{k=0}^{n-1} (\mathbf{v}_{ik} - \mathbf{v}'_{ik})^2\right)^{\frac{1}{2}} \tag{1}$$

Various clustering algorithms have been proposed, e.g. DBSCAN [23]. DBSCAN finds clusters based on a density measure, i.e., it finds clusters in which data instances have only a maximal distance to each other. Hence, points near to each other are grouped in the same cluster. This may lead to arbitrary shaped clusters, including spherical cluster shapes. On the one hand, arbitrary shaped clusters do not lead to any clear results, and on the other hand, clusters in our case might have varying density values ϵ, which is problematic for DBSCAN. The algorithm of our choice is fixed-width clustering [9, 24]. The algorithm, described in Figure 3, has the benefit of a better runtime complexity, compared to other clustering algorithms, e.g., standard k-means, since it computes clusters with just a single passage through the data instances (fingerprints). In fixed-width clustering, clusters have a maximal width and a cluster center, called centroid. Data instances that are clustered based on their feature vector either surpass the maximal width (based on the distance measure) and create a new cluster or have a smaller distance and become part of the cluster and have a certain distance to its centroid. The fewer data instances are inside a cluster the more probable it is that those data instances are in fact outliers. This is basically the assumption discussed before: *normal behaviour represents the majority of data instances whereas abnormal behaviour is represented by only few data instances* (which represent potential attacks). Hence, clusters containing fewer instances than a user-configured threshold, represent anomalous data points. For instance if less than 1% of data instances are within a cluster it is labeled as anomalous. We leverage the distance notation from Formula 1 to $d(\mathbf{v}_i, C)$ to denote the distance from a feature vector to a cluster (represented by its centroid). The algorithm to cluster the fingerprints, as described in [24, 9], consists of 3 steps:

1. The set S of clusters is first initialized to the empty set.
2. A fingerprint $\mathbf{v}_i = (\mathbf{v}_i, \ldots, \mathbf{v}_{in-1})$ is taken from the set of fingerprints (unlabeled set of fingerprints).
   IF The set S is still empty then the fingerprint will create a new cluster C and $\mathbf{v}_i$ will be the centroid.
   ELSE The cluster C with the smallest distance is selected $\arg\min_{C \in S}(d(\mathbf{v}_i, C))$ such that the fingerprint does not surpass the maximal width. If such a cluster is found, the fingerprint is inserted, otherwise a new cluster is generated and $\mathbf{v}_i$ will be the centroid.
3. The second step is repeated for all remaining fingerprints.

Fig. 3. Clustering as described in [24, 9]

Detecting Abnormal Entities and False-Positives. Clusters containing less fingerprints than the user-specified threshold are automatically labeled as outliers. The fingerprints within, and their entities they represent, are then also labeled as anomalous. For each entity there are two possibilities for creating an anomaly alert, (i) either through a change of behaviour from itself, or (ii) by being substantially different from other entities of the same type. The idea behind (i) is that the system collects fingerprints for a single entity over an amount of time, i.e., hours or months, and clusters them. If an entity did not change its behaviour, its fingerprints are in the same dense cluster c. The more changes an entity undergoes (stored in the behavioural profile) the more the fingerprints change. Eventually the generated fingerprint surpasses the distance to the centroid of c and results in an anomaly alert. In case of (ii) fingerprints are used to compare entities among each other. A user, who exhibits a significant different usage pattern, creates his own cluster and is labeled as anomalous. In case a new user, service, or host is introduced to the system, it can be determined automatically if said entity is abnormal or not, simply by comparing its fingerprint.

Through the use of the domain model, entities are put in relation to each other, i.e., users to hosts, or services to workflows. Anomalies are, thus, put into context and alerts propagated upwards. For instance, abnormal services, hosts, and users, determine the security status of the assigned workflows. Vice-versa, drilling down on an abnormal workflow (e.g., too much network traffic or too many document queries), exposes abnormal entities, e.g., anomalous services, users, hosts, and speeds-up root-cause analysis.

It is possible, even likely, that some clusters that are detected anomalous are actually not anomalous. Groups of fileservers will, for instance, have different fingerprints than mail servers or timeservers. It is therefore important to consider various degrees of optimization to prevent false-positives. There are a couple of options, since the clustering algorithm is parameterized by two variables,

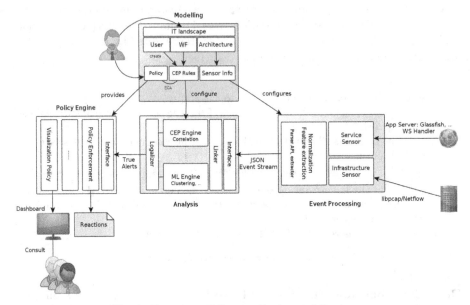

Fig. 4. Overview of the monitoring architecture

the width and the threshold for anomalies, tweaking either of them will reduce false-positives. An increased cluster-width allows sparse clusters, exhibiting a significant higher variance, to be normal. Rising the threshold allows to have clusters with few instances to be normal as well. Another option is the creation of tests to determine the true state of an entity, but that is left for future work. If a cluster, and the ensuing entities within, are still labeled as anomalies the framework provides to relabel them as normal.

3   Architecture

Figure 4 indicates the different components of our monitoring architecture, which can be offered by a cloud provider as a *Monitoring as a Service* solution. A tenant uses the DSL provided by the *modeling component* to provide a model which describes his IT landscape. This model is aligned to the three layers we discussed above. Based on the model, rules to detect workflow non-compliance are created to configure the CEP engine. To customize the monitoring service, the tenant supplies the *policy engine* with policies (which are rules or metrics) to enable the cloud provider to react on alerts. Policies specify (i) the gravity of alerts and (ii) what should happen in case they happen. By providing a policy, a tenant bids the cloud provider to cut off a virtual host from the network, if said host is classified as an information leaking host. This state can be mantained until the host is classified as normal. The *event processing* component consists of service and network sensors as well as a normalization feature extraction element. The sensors act as event sinks for multiple service and network event emitter sources. The service sensor receives JSON[10] encoded service call data, whereas the network monitor is built as a netflow-collector. Analysis of workflow compliance (i.e. via CEP) and outlier detection (i.e., via Clustering) is done in the *analysis component*. Statistical methods, i.e., z-scores are computed by "The Apache Commons Mathematics Library".[11] The CEP engine of choice is ESPER[12]. Based on the outcome of the analysis and the severity of alerts, the policy engine populates the *dashboard* and determines reactive measures for the cloud provider (policies provided by the tenant). The dashboard displays integral information about a tenant's infrastructure, i.e., the infrastructure in tabular form, important alerts, and anomalous entities.

4   Related Work

In this section we discuss related work in the areas of cloud security monitoring, anomaly detection, and CEP. In the area of cloud security monitoring several related papers have been published, yet among those [25] seems the most related. Vieira et al. [25] focus on distributed architectures in grid and cloud computing and perform behavioural analysis via neural networks. [25] leverage neural networks for behavioural analysis we use clustering. Moreover the anomalies we find are disjoint from theirs. There has been plenty of research for anomaly detection via clustering, a survey on this topic is provided by [8]. Clustering is quite versatile as the approaches in [9, 24, 10, 12] point out. Portnoy et al. [9] detect attacks, e.g., denial of service, in the KDD 1999 data via clustering of network activity set.[13] Gu et al. [12] use clustering for the detection of botnets by a framework called "Botminer". The Authors in [10] improve clustering for NIDS by using a density-based clustering algorithm and a grid-based metric and evaluate their efforts on the KDD 1999 data set. To measure hosts we create profiles of their network behaviour by sampling their TCP/UDP flows based on [26, 12]. To our knowledge, the clustering algorithm itself was first presented in [9]. Instead of clustering individual multi-dimensional features form the KDD training set we cluster fingerprints of various entities. The main difference from the proposed work of Gu et al. [12] is that the former only profiles hosts for the specific detection of botnets, whereas we only try to find outliers and assemble outliers in a holistic profile of the infrastructure. The approach presented in [26] is more similar to ours since it also profiles machines in the network. But we're not restricted to machines only, but also services, users, and workflows.

The multi-tier DSL proposed in this paper allows the definition of node hierarchies, roles, actors, and distinguishes three layers. These design decisions are in its core similar to [14, 15]. Breu and Innerhofer et al. provide a model-based approach with concepts for security management. There is related work for DSLs

---

[10] http://www.json.org/, Accessed: July 30, 2012.

[11] http://commons.apache.org/math/, Accessed: July 30, 2012.

[12] http://esper.codehaus.org/, Accessed: July 20, 2012.

[13] http://kdd.ics.uci.edu/databases/kddcup99/kddcup99.html, Accessed: July 20, 2012.

to create service infrastructures Berre et al. [27] present the *Service Oriented Architecture Modeling Language (SoaML)* and Popescu et al. provide the *Service Markup Language* SML. SoaML was not desireable for our scenario, since our interest was more cloud oriented than SOA-centric. Our DSL allows the definition of event-sequences, which in turn allow to detect deviances to rules generated by the workflow model. The paradigm of modeling services as events is similar to event-driven process chains (EPC), discussed in-depth in [28]. Workflow compliance in SOA via CEP has been discussed by Mulo et al. [16]. A service invocation is regarded as an event and business process activities as event-trails. These event-trails guide the creation of queries which a CEP engine uses to identify and monitor business activities. Anomaly detection itself has been done frequently in many domains, though to the best of our knowledge, there is no cloud monitoring approach that allows CEP and anomaly detection to monitor (a) the execution of workflows for semantic gaps and (b) detect infrastructure anomalies relative to said workflows. Due to the formal representation of "behaviour" of entities we're able to pinpoint suspicious services, users, hosts, and workflows.

5   Conclusion and Future Work

We have sketched a context-based anomaly detection framework to facilitate real-time monitoring of cloud-sourced workflows and infrastructures. Our research differs from existing monitoring work as we aim to mitigate cloud threat-scenarios with web services and infrastructure anomaly detection, and CEP. The framework aims to keep multiple profiles of entities on various layers and to link detected anomalies and semantic gaps to workflows. Future work will consist of,

- An implementation and an evaluation based on a real-world scenario. The planned evaluation will consist of a real-life healthcare scenario where services, data, and hosts, are outsourced to an IaaS cloud. The architecture consists of all services necessary to allow a regulated flow of action in a hospital, e.g., image retrieval services, diagnose services, and an XACML-Kerberos like access control infrastructure. Based on the runtime behaviour of the system we train our machine-learning component and measure deviations of user- and network-activity. To measure the effectiveness of our approach the healthcare architecture will be subject to various use cases/attacks, i.e., a failed XACML architecture, leak attacks from insiders, fuzzy security-testing of web-services from other tenants, or TCP/UDP malware propagation across the cloud. The evaluation will show if the anomaly detection can provide information about these attacks.
- Carefully evaluating other clustering methods, e.g., Entropy Maximization, to reduce false-positives and attain a better clustering result.
- A CEP rule repository to further allow the reduction of false-positives with domain knowledge, detect additional signature-based events to augment the profiles for entities in general. Along the way goes the inclusion of other

monitoring tools such as Snort[14] and Ossec[15] to get a more elaborate profile for hosts.

- Finding anomalies is a good first step, but it serves a wider purpose, i.e., the semi-automatic labeling of clusters via supervised learning. First, normal and anomalous clusters are labeled, then based on the fingerprints in these clusters training data for supervised learning, e.g., Naive-Bayes, Random Forests, is easily generated. New fingerprints can then be readily classified as a specific form of behaviour.

References

1. Amazon, EC: Amazon elastic compute cloud (amazon ec2). Amazon Elastic Compute Cloud, Amazon EC2 (2010)
2. Armbrust, M., Fox, A., Griffith, R., Joseph, A., Katz, R., Konwinski, A., Lee, G., Patterson, D., Rabkin, A., Stoica, I., et al.: A view of cloud computing. Communications of the ACM 53(4), 50–58 (2010)
3. Ristenpart, T., Tromer, E., Shacham, H., Savage, S.: Hey, you, get off of my cloud: exploring information leakage in third-party compute clouds. In: Proceedings of the 16th ACM Conference on Computer and Communications Security, pp. 199–212. ACM (2009)
4. Walker-Morgan, D.: Vsftpd backdoor discovered in source code. Website (2011), http://h-online.com/-1272310 (visited: July 4, 2011)
5. Hoglund, G., Butler, J.: Rootkits: subverting the Windows kernel. Addison-Wesley Professional (2006)
6. Koziol, J.: Intrusion Detection with Snort, 1st edn. Sams, Indianapolis (2003)
7. Trend Micro, Inc.: Ossec documentation, http://www.ossec.net/ (accessed: December 14, 2010)
8. Garcia-Teodoro, P., Diaz-Verdejo, J., Macia-Fernandez, G., Vazquez, E.: Anomaly-based Network Intrusion Detection: Techniques, Systems and Challenges. Computers & Security 28(1-2), 18–28 (2009)
9. Portnoy, L., Eskin, E., Stolfo, S.: Intrusion detection with unlabeled data using clustering. In: Proceedings of ACM CSS Workshop on Data Mining Applied to Security (2001)
10. Leung, K., Leckie, C.: Unsupervised anomaly detection in network intrusion detection using clusters. In: Proceedings of the Twenty-eighth Australasian Conference on Computer Science, vol. 38, pp. 333–342 (2005)
11. Chandola, V., Banerjee, A., Kumar, V.: Anomaly detection: A survey. ACM Computing Surveys (CSUR) 41(3), 15 (2009)
12. Gu, G., Perdisci, R., Zhang, J., Lee, W.: Botminer: clustering analysis of network traffic for protocol-and structure-independent botnet detection. In: Proceedings of the 17th Conference on Security Symposium, pp. 139–154 (2008)
13. Eckert, M., Bry, F.: Complex Event Processing, CEP (2009)
14. Breu, R., Innerhofer-Oberperfler, F., Yautsiukhin, A.: Quantitative assessment of enterprise security system. In: The Third International Conference on Availability, Reliability and Security, pp. 921–928. IEEE (2008)

---

[14] http://www.snort.org/, Accessed: July 30, 2012.

[15] http://www.ossec.net/, Accessed: July 30, 2012.

15. Innerhofer-Oberperfler, F., Breu, R., Hafner, M.: Living security collaborative security management in a changing world. In: Parallel and Distributed Computing and Networks/720: Software Engineering. ACTA Press (2011)
16. Mulo, E., Zdun, U., Dustdar, S.: Monitoring web service event trails for business compliance. In: 2009 IEEE International Conference on Service-Oriented Computing and Applications (SOCA), pp. 1–8. IEEE (2009)
17. Grohe, S., Schlameu, C., Sommer, R.: Performancevergleich von cep-engines. Technical report, Hochschulschriftenserver der Universitt Stuttgart, Germany (2010), http://elib.uni-stuttgart.de/opus/oai2/oai2.php
18. Denning, D.: An intrusion-detection model. IEEE Transactions on Software Engineering (2), 222–232 (1987)
19. Durgin, N.A., Zhang, P.: Profile-based adaptive anomaly detection for network security (2005)
20. Nicolett, M., Kelly, K.: 2012 Gartner Critical Capabilities and Magic Quadrant for SIEM (2012)
21. Tan, P., Steinbach, M., Kumar, V.: Cluster Analysis: basic concepts and algorithms. In: Introduction to Data Mining. Addison-Wensley (2006)
22. Finch, H.: Comparison of distance measures in cluster analysis with dichotomous data. Journal of Data Science 3(1), 85–100 (2005)
23. Ester, M., Kriegel, H., Sander, J., Xu, X.: A density-based algorithm for discovering clusters in large spatial databases with noise. In: Proceedings of the 2nd International Conference on Knowledge Discovery and Data Mining, vol. 1996, pp. 226–231. AAAI Press (1996)
24. Oldmeadow, J., Ravinutala, S., Leckie, C.: Adaptive clustering for network intrusion detection. In: Dai, H., Srikant, R., Zhang, C. (eds.) PAKDD 2004. LNCS (LNAI), vol. 3056, pp. 255–259. Springer, Heidelberg (2004)
25. Vieira, K., Schulter, A., Westphall, C., Westphall, C.: Intrusion detection for grid and cloud computing. IT Professional 12(4), 38–43 (2010)
26. Hernandez-Campos, F., Nobel, A., Smith, F., Jeffay, K.: Understanding patterns of tcp connection usage with statistical clustering. In: 13th IEEE International Symposium on Modeling, Analysis, and Simulation of Computer and Telecommunication Systems, pp. 35–44. IEEE (2005)
27. Berre, A.: Service oriented architecture modeling language (soaml)-specification for the uml profile and metamodel for services, upms (2008)
28. van der Aalst, W.: Formalization and verification of event-driven process chains. Information and Software Technology 41(10), 639–650 (1999)

Using Machine Learning and Information Retrieval Techniques to Improve Software Maintainability*

Anna Corazza[1], Sergio Di Martino[1], Valerio Maggio[1],
Alessandro Moschitti[2], Andrea Passerini[2],
Giuseppe Scanniello[3], and Fabrizio Silvestri[4]

[1] University of Naples "Federico II", Italy
[2] University of Trento, Italy
[3] University of Basilicata, Italy
[4] ISTI Institute - CNR, Italy

Abstract. In this paper, we investigate some ideas based on Machine Learning, Natural Language Processing, and Information Retrieval to outline possible research directions in the field of software architecture recovery and clone detection. In particular, after presenting an extensive related work, we illustrate two proposals for addressing these two issues, that represent hot topics in the field of Software Maintenance. Both proposals use Kernel Methods for exploiting structural representation of source code and to automate the detection of clones and the recovery of the actually implemented architecture in a subject software system.

Keywords: Information Retrieval, Natural Language Processing, Machine Learning, Software Maintenance and Evolution.

1 Introduction

Software maintenance is an essential step in the evolution of software systems and represents one of the most expensive, time consuming, and challenging phases of the whole development process. As declared in Lehman's laws of Software Evolution [31], a software system must be continuously adapted during its overall life cycle or it progressively becomes less satisfactory (*Lehman's first law*). Thus, as software applications are doomed to evolve and grow [13], all of the applied changes and adaptations inevitably reduce their quality (*Lehman's second law*).

According to Garlan [18], architectural information represents an important resource for software maintainers to aid the comprehension, the analysis, and the maintenance of large and complex systems. In fact, software architectures

---

* The research described in this paper has been partially supported by the European Community's Seventh Framework Programme (FP7/2007-2013) under the grants #247758: ETERNALS – Trustworthy Eternal Systems via Evolving Software, Data and Knowledge, and #288024: LiMoSINE – Linguistically Motivated Semantic aggregation engiNes.

A. Moschitti and B. Plank (Eds.): EternalS 2013, CCIS 379, pp. 117–134, 2013.

provide *models* and *views* representing the relationships among different software components according to a particular set of concerns [13]. However, unlike classes or packages, this information do not have an explicit representation in the source code. Moreover, the external documentation is usually not present nor updated. Therefore, the existing code remains the most updated source of information to exploit in order to automatically retrieve and reconstruct the architecture of a software system. Several approaches have been proposed in the literature to support this task, known as *Software Architecture Recovery* (SAR) [13]. Many of these techniques derive *architectural views* of the subject system from the source code by applying some clustering analysis techniques to software artifacts, considered at different levels of granularity (e.g., at *classes* level) [13]. In this scenario, one of the challenges is to define a proper similarity measure among software artifacts in order to exploit their representation and to group together the most related ones.

Another well known and largely investigated issue in software maintenance is clone detection: it is focused on the identification of source code duplications. Software clones might affect the reliability and the maintainability of large software systems. For example, errors affecting a fragment of code must be fixed in everyone of its possible duplications. In general, duplications in source code is a phenomenon that occurs frequently in large software systems [3]. Reasons why programmers duplicate code are manifold. The most well known is a common bad programming practice, i.e., copying and pasting [40], that gives rise to *software clones*, or simply *clones*. However, in addition to simply copying and pasting fragments of code, programmers usually adapt software copies to the new context by applying multiple modifications (e.g., adding new statements and renaming variables). Thus, similarly to SAR, the computation of the similarity between source code becomes crucial [40].

In this paper, we explore the possibility to combine different methods gathered from Information Retrieval (IR), Natural Language Processing (NLP) and Machine Learning (ML) fields to automatically mine information from the source code for the identification of clones and the recovery of the actually implemented architecture in a subject software. In particular, we investigate the application of Kernel Methods [20,37] to define similarity measures able to exploit the structural representation of the source code. We used these techniques in the fields of architecture reconstruction and clone detection because they provide flexible solutions able to analyze large data set with reasonable computational requirements.

Paper Structure. In Sections 2 and 3, we provide an extensive state-of-the-art for SAR and clone detection techniques respectively. In Section 4, we illustrate our proposal for clone detection. Section 5 describes the case study used in the evaluation procedure, whose results are reported in Section 6. Plans for applying kernel machines and advanced structured-output learning approaches for SAR are discussed in Section 7. Finally, conclusions are drawn in Section 8.

2 State-of-the-Art in Automatic SAR

A complete and extensive survey of SAR techniques is proposed by Ducasse et al. [13] where authors provide an accurate taxonomy of different approaches according to five distinct aspects, namely the *goals*, the *process*, the *inputs*, the *techniques* and the *outputs*. In this paper, we limit our analysis only to approaches of automatic SAR for the clustering of functional (sub)modules.

The definition of effective methods to automatically partition systems into meaningful subsystems, requires that several non trivial issues are considered [26]: *(i)* the level of granularity for the software entities considered in the clustering; *(ii)* the information used to compare software entities, and *(iii)* the clustering algorithm adopted to group similar artifacts. In Table 1 summarizes the state of the art regarding software clustering for the recovery of software architectures.

Table 1. Overview of architecture recovery approaches

Approach	Used Information	Clustering Algorithm	Automatic or Semi-automatic
Anquetil and Lethbridge [1]	structural	hierarchical	semi-automatic
Mitchell and Mancoridis [36]	structural	hill climbing	automatic
Doval et al. [12]	structural	genetic algorithms	automatic
Bittencourt and Guerrero [5]	structural	edge betweenness; k-means; modul. quality; design structure matrix	semi-automatic
Wu *et al.* [47]	structural	hierarchical; prog. compreh. patterns; Bunch	semi-automatic
Tzerpos and Holt [43]	structural	hierarchical	semi-automatic
Kuhn et al. [29]	lexical	hierarchical	semi-automatic
Risi et al. [38]	lexical	k-means	automatic
Corazza et al. [8,7,10]	lexical	k-medoids; hierarchical	automatic
Maqbool and Babri [34]	lexical structural	hierarchical	semi-automatic
Maletic and Marcus [33]	lexical structural	minimum spanning tree	semi-automatic
Scanniello et al. [42]	lexical structural	k-means	automatic

To better provide a detailed overview of different approaches, in the following we present the related literature with respect to the information exploited in the clustering process, namely structural information, lexical information, and their combinations.

Structural Based Approaches: The works proposed by Wiggerts [46] and by Anquetil and Lethbridge [1] represent the first two contributions to semi-automatic approaches for the clustering of software entities. In particular, in [1] authors present a comparative study of different hierarchical clustering algorithms based on structural information. However the proposed solutions require human decisions (e.g., cutting points of the dendrograms) to get the best partition of software entities into clusters.

Maqbool and Babri in [34] highlight the features of hierarchical clustering research in the context of software architecture recovery. Special emphasis is posed on the analysis of different similarity and distance measures that could be effectively used in clustering software artifacts. The main contribution of the paper is, however, the analysis of two clustering based approaches and their experimental assessment. The discussed approaches try to reduce the number of decisions to be taken during the clustering. They also conducted an empirical evaluation of the clustering based approaches on four large software systems.

Mitchell and Mancoridis in [36] present a novel clustering algorithm, named *Bunch*. Bunch produces system decompositions applying search based techniques in combination with several heuristics, such as the *coupling* and *cohesion* of produced partitions, specifically designed for the clustering of software artifacts. In particular, the coupling and the cohesion heuristics are defined in terms of *intra-* e *inter-* clusters dependencies respectively. The evaluation of the produced partitions has been conducted according to qualitative and quantitative empirical investigations. Similarly, Dove et al. [12] propose a structural approach based on genetic algorithms to group software entities in clusters.

Clustering algorithms based on structural information have also been used in the analysis of the software architecture evolution [5], [47]. Wu et al. in [47] present a comparative study of a number of clustering algorithms: *(a)* hierarchical agglomerative clustering algorithms based on the Jaccard coefficient and the single/complete linkage update rules; *(b)* an algorithm based on program comprehension patterns that tries to recover subsystems that are commonly found in manually-created decompositions of large software systems; and *(c)* a customized configuration of an algorithm implemented in Bunch [36]. Similarly, Bittencourt and Guerrero [5] present an empirical study to evaluate four widely known clustering algorithms on a number of software systems implemented in Java and C/C++. The analyzed algorithms are: Edge betweenness clustering, k-means clustering, modularization quality clustering, and design structure matrix clustering.

Lexical Based Approaches: Software clustering approaches exploiting lexical information are based on the idea that the lexicon provided by developers in the source code represent a key source of information. In particular, such techniques mine relevant information from source code identifiers and comments based on the assumption that related artifacts are those that share the same vocabulary.

The approach proposed by Kuhn et al. [29] constitutes one of the first proposals in this direction defining an automatic technique based on the application of the Latent Semantic Indexing (LSI) method [11]. The approach is language independent and mines the lexical information gathered from source code comments. In addition, the approach enables software engineers to identify topics in the source code by means of labeling of the identified clusters.

Similarly, Risi et al. [38] propose an approach that uses the LSI and the k-means clustering algorithm to form groups of software entities that implement similar functionality. A variant based on fold-in and fold-out is introduced as well. Furthermore this proposal provides an important contribution on the analysis of computational costs necessary to assess the validity of a clustering process.

Corazza et al. [8] propose a clustering based approach that considers the source code text as structured in different zones providing different relevance of information. In particular, the relevance of each zone is automatically weighted thanks to the definition of a probabilistic generative model and the application of the Expectation-Maximization (EM) algorithm. Related artifacts are then grouped accordingly using a customization of the k-medoids clustering algorithm. More recently the same authors propose an investigation on the effectiveness of the EM algorithm in combination with different code zones [7] and different clustering algorithms [10].

Structural and Lexical Based Approaches: Maletic and Marcus in [33] propose an approach based on the combination of lexical and structural information to support comprehension tasks within the maintenance and reengineering of software systems. From the lexical point of view they consider problem and development domains. On the other hand, the structural dimension refers to the actual syntactic structure of the program along with the control and dataflow that it represents. Software entities are compared using LSI, while file organization is used to get structural information. To group programs in clusters a simple graph theoretic algorithm is used. The algorithm takes as input an undirected graph (the graph obtained computing the cosine similarity of the two vector representations of all the source code documents) and then constructs a Minimal Spanning Tree (MST). Clusters are identified pruning the edges of the MST with a weight larger than a given threshold. To assess the effectiveness of the approach some case studies on a version of Mosaic are presented and discussed.

Scanniello et al. [42] present a two phase approach for recovering hierarchical software architectures of object oriented software systems. The first phase uses structural information to identify software layers [41]. To this end, a customization of the Kleinberg algorithm [24] is used. The second phase uses lexical information extracted from the source code to identify similarity among pairs of classes and then partitions each identified layer into software modules. The main limitation of this approach is that it is only suitable for software systems exhibiting a classical tiered architecture.

3   State-of-the-Art of Clone Detection Techniques

In this section we summarize research in the area of clone detection, grouping the proposals according to the features they exploit to identify similarities among software artifacts. Note that our goal here is not to provide an extensive analysis of the clone detection approaches presented in the literature but to provide an overview of most important techniques together with a general background on the problem, necessary to introduce the proposal presented in Section 4. An exhaustive survey of clone detection tools and techniques is provided in [40].

Table 2. Overview of clone detection techniques

Approach	Used Information	Technique
Ducasse et al. [14] Johnson [22]	Textual	String matching
Baker [2] Kamiya et al. [23]	Token	Pattern matching Suffix-tree matching
Yang [48] Baxter et al. [3] Koschke et al. [27] Bulychev et al. [6] Jiang et al. [21]	Syntactic	Dynamic Programming Tree Matching Suffix-tree AST Anti-unification (NLP) LSH
Komondoor and Horwitz [25] Krinke [28] Gabel et al. [17]	Structural	PDG Slicing PDG Heuristics PDG Slicing
Leitão [32] Wahler et al. [45] Corazza et al. [9] Roy and Cordy [39]	Combined	Software metrics Frequent Item-sets Tree Kernels (ML) Code Transformation

Textual Based Approaches: Ducasse et al. [14] propose a language-independent approach to detect code clones, based on line-based string matching and visual presentation of the cloned code. A different approach is presented by Johnson [22] where the author applies a string matching technique based on fingerprints to identify exact repetitions of text in the source code of large software systems.

The main feature of these techniques relies in their efficiency and scalability, easily applicable to the analysis of large software systems. However, their detection capabilities are very limited and only restricted to very similar textual duplications (line by line). As a matter of fact these approaches are scarcely usable in practice.

Token Based Approaches: Baker [2] suggests an approach to identify duplications and near-duplications (i.e., copies with slightly modifications) in large software systems. The proposed approach finds source code copies that are substantially the same except for global substitutions. Similarly, Kamiya et al. [23]

use a suffix-tree matching algorithm to compute token-by-token matching among source code fragments. The authors adopt optimization techniques that mainly normalize token sequences. This is due to the fact that the underlying algorithm may be expensive when used on large software systems. The main drawback of these approaches is that they completely disregard the syntactic structure of the analyzed source code, similarly to textual based techniques. As a consequence, these solutions may detect a large number of false clones, usually not corresponding to any actual syntactic unit.

Syntactic Based Approaches: Syntactic based approaches exploit the information provided by Abstract Syntax Trees (AST) to identify similar code fragments. Such techniques are more robust to modifications in code fragments than textual and token based technique. However, they may possibly fail in case modifications concerns the inversion or the substitution of entire code blocks: the so-called *gapped-clones* [28]. Yang [48] uses dynamic programming to find differences between two versions of the same source file. A similar approach is presented by Baxter et al. [3]. It is based on a tree matching algorithm to compare sub-trees of an AST of a given software system. On the other hand, Koschke et al. [27] describe an approach to detect clones based on suffix trees of serialized ASTs. The main contribution of this work is that software clones can be identified in linear time and space. A different approach is presented by Bulychev et al. [6], where authors propose a clone detection technique based on the *anti-unification* algorithm, widely used in Natural Language processing tasks. A novel approach for detecting similar trees has been presented by Jiang et al. [21] in their tool *Deckard*. In their approach, certain characteristic vectors are computed to approximate the structure of ASTs in a Euclidean space. Locality sensitive hashing (LSH) is then used to cluster similar vectors using the Euclidean distance metric.

Structural Based Approaches: Structural based approaches gather information from control and dependency graphs to identify clones. In particular these techniques apply algorithms to identify isomorphic sub-graphs within a graph built considering control and data flow dependencies (i.e., the program dependence graphs, PDG) of the software system to analyze. Komondoor and Horwitz [25] propose an approach based on program slicing techniques, applied on PDGs. On the other hand, Krinke [28] propose a heuristic based approach to identify isomorphic sub-graphs. More recently, Gabel et al. [17] propose a PDG-based technique that maps slices of PDGs to syntax subtrees and applies the Deckard clone detection tool [21]. The main advantage of these techniques is that they do not depend on the particular textual representation of the code, allowing to detect also functional duplications, in addition to the textual based ones considered by previous approaches. However the identification of isomorphic sub-graphs is a NP-hard problem and only approximated solutions may be provided.

Combined Approaches: In the literature techniques that combine different artifacts representation have been defined. For example, Leitão [32] combines syntactic and semantic techniques using functions that consider various aspects of software systems (e.g., similar call sub-graphs, commutative operators, user-defined equivalences). Differently, Wahler et al. [45] present an approach based on a data mining technique to detect clones. This approach uses the concept of frequent item-sets on the XML representation of the software system to be analyzed. Finally, Roy and Cordy [39] present an approach based on source transformations and text line comparison to find clones.

4   Clone Detection

As briefly introduced in the previous Section, the definition of clones [3] states that two code fragments form a clone if they are "similar" according to some definition of similarity. However, such similarity can be based on the program text, on the implemented functionality (independent of the text), or on both. In the literature, all these kinds of code similarities correspond to the following taxonomy of clones [40]:

Type 1 : An exact copy of consecutive code fragments without modifications (except for white spaces and comments).

Type 2 : Syntactically identical fragments except for variations in identifiers, literals, and variable types in addition to Type-1 variations;

Type 3 : Copied fragments with further modifications such as changed, added, or deleted statements in addition to Type-2 variations.

Type 4 : Code fragments that perform similar functionality but are implemented by different syntactic variants.

According to this classification, only Type 1 clones are represented by exactly the same set of instructions, while the other three types involve lexical and syntactic variations between the two fragments. As a consequence, an effective similarity measure has to combine both the syntactic and lexical information in order to produce a correct solution. Therefore, the input representation is the first crucial point to consider when designing a Machine Learning-based clone detector. In addition, annotated data are needed to train the considered techniques. These two points will be discussed in depth in the remainder of this section.

4.1   Code Similarities and Kernel Methods

Kernel Methods [20] have shown to be effective in approaches considering the similarity between complex input structures. In particular, Tree Kernels have been widely used in fields where the information is represented by means of tree-based structures, like Natural Language Processing [37] and Bioinformatics [44], where they have been applied to Parse- and Phylogenetic-trees respectively. When dealing with the clone detection problem, an interesting solution could be to apply Tree Kernels to Abstract Syntax Trees (ASTs) of the source code, as proposed by Corazza et al. [9]. In particular, since the sole syntactic information is not sufficient to decide whether two code fragments are clones or not, the authors proposed to enrich the information present in each (internal) node of the AST by annotating them with the *lexemes* gathered from the corresponding leaf nodes. Authors reported a formal definition of such Tree Kernel function for clone detection, together with its experimental evaluation. Results showed that the Tree Kernel approach applied on modified ASTs is able to outperform a purely AST-based technique in detecting up to Type 3 clones [9].

The main drawback of this approach is that it could not be effectively applied in the identification of Type 4 clones, as the definition of similarity it embeds mainly considers the program text of the compared code fragments. Conversely, to deal with Type 4 clones, the information about the *program behavior* becomes particularly relevant. As a matter of fact, most of the clone detection techniques that are able to detect Type 4 clones [28,25,17] use Program Dependency Graphs (PDGs) to represent the source code. In a PDG, nodes correspond to simple statements and control flow predicates, and edges encode data and control dependencies [17].

To this aim, we are currently investigating the opportunity to apply Graph Kernels to PDGs, to detect meaningful similar subgraphs. However, the main limitation of such approaches regards the computational effort they require, which is in fact much larger than what is needed by Tree Kernels. Thus, to find a good trade-off between such cost and the information considered in the (sub)graphs comparison, we are focusing on the application of Weighted Decomposition Kernels (WDK) [35] as they enable to define specific criteria to reduce the total number of comparisons.

4.2   Automatic Generation of Training Data

A typical problem in developing Machine Learning approaches regards the necessity to arrange two different sets of annotated data, namely the training and the assessment sets. This problem is particularly important in the case of clone detection where these labeled data sets are even more difficult than usual to produce, since a manual annotation of large systems is infeasible. The generally adopted solution to this problem considers the definition of a *pooling process*, such as the one described in [4], where a limited set of results, gathered from different clone detection tools, is manually cross-checked. However, the effect of such a procedure is that there is no guarantee of completeness and so only an underestimation of the actual performance can be provided. In addition to that, these data are not so effective for training new algorithms, since they present a bias towards the clones detected by the solutions used to produce the data set.

In this scenario, only unsupervised Machine Learning, i.e. clustering, can be proposed. However, clustering can not be expected to be accurate enough for this application, as the learning process is only guided by the similarity computation.

As an alternative, we propose to construct the training data by simulation, and then to use them to train a classifier for clone detection. The simulation process artificially produces clones by modifying parts of the input project and injects them by following predefined probability distributions. In this way, the quality of the training set can be controlled without any need of imposing restrictions on its size. A Kernel-based classifier is then trained on this data set.

To this aim, we designed and implemented an algorithm able to inject clones in the source code. In particular this algorithm would allow us to automatically generate a training set and to apply a more reliable strategy in the definition of the supervised Kernel learning process. The main core of our clone injection algorithm is represented by the function InjectClone, whose Pseudocode is reported in Algorithm 1. This algorithm is able to generate function clones and to track their location in the source code, thus obtaining a labeled dataset of clones of the given input Type.

In more details, the algorithm starts its computation by parsing the stream of source code of the analyzed software system in order to extract all the target functions (Line 2). Afterwards each function is processed one at a time, deciding whether or not it has to be cloned (Line 6) and how many clones should be generated (Line 9). In particular, we consider that each function has a probability probCloning of being cloned. Moreover, if a function has to be cloned, the number of clones to generate is randomly chosen according to a geometric probability distribution with parameter 0.5, namely $\Pr(\text{nCopies}) = 0.5^n$ (Lines 9 - 11).

Finally, the algorithm invokes the procedures Clone and Inject to perform the generation and the injection of clones in the source code respectively, and returns the tracking info of generated data.

The Pseudocode of the Clone procedure is reported in Algorithm 2.

The Clone procedure is able to perform the generation of clones up to Type 4 by employing a set of different procedures to apply specific modifications to the program text (mutation) of the target function. The invocation of such procedures is performed in accordance with the Type of the clone to generate. We are not reporting the Pseudocode of such functions in the current document due to space limitations.

The first mutation operation is performed by the CopyAndChangeLayout function (Line 2) that is always applied to the target function, regardless the selected clone Type. This is because all the four definitions of clones allow some modification in the layout of the program text. The substitution of identifiers and literals is performed for Type 2 clones up to Type 4 ones, by invoking the SubstituteIdsAndLiterals procedure (Line 4). In particular, such procedure processes every literal and identifiers of the input function, each of which has a probability probSubstituteId of being substituted with a randomly generated identifier.

When dealing with Type 3 clones, in addition to mutations applied for Type 2, other additional operations should be considered. Indeed, in a Type 3 clone, two fragments of code may differ also in the statements, that could be added or removed (Line 7). Therefore, we assigned the same probability (i.e., 1/2 for each operation) to the insertion of a new statement randomly extracted from the considered software system and the deletion of a statement. Furthermore, we impose an upper bound to the total number of operations which is a randomly

Algorithm 1. Clone Injection Algorithm

Require: sourceCode : Source code of the system under analysis;
Require: type : Type of the clones to generate;
Require: probCloning: (Constant) The probability of functions/methods to be cloned.
Ensure: The source code of the system with randomly injected clones;
Ensure: The tracking info of injected clones in the source code.

```
 1: function InjectClones(sourceCode, type)
 2:     functionList ← parseAndExtractFunctionsFrom(sourceCode)
 3:     clonesTrackInfo ← ∅
 4:     for each: function ∈ functionList do
 5:         probGenerateClone ← random(0,1)
 6:         if probGenerateClone ≤ probCloning then
 7:             nCopies ← 0
 8:             dice ← random(0, 1)
 9:             while not (2^{-(nCopies+1)} ≤ dice ≤ 2^{-nCopies}) do
10:                 nCopies ← nCopies + 1
11:             end while
12:             for i = 1 to nCopies do
13:                 newClone ← Clone(function, type)
14:                 trackInfo ← Inject(sourceCode, newClone)
15:                 add(clonesTrackInfo, trackInfo)
16:             end for
17:         end if
18:     end for
19:     return clonesTrackInfo
20: end function
```

---

generated fraction of the total number of statements in the analyzed function. In this way, we may avoid the generation of a totally different function which will not be an actual clone of the target one.

Finally, in case of Type 4 clones, the mutation operations include the reordering of statements (Line 9) and the replacement of equivalent control structures (Line 10). In particular the former is applied only to declaration and independent statements, while the latter substitutes possibly occurring control structures with other semantically equivalent. For instance, for loops may be replaced with while loops, as well as if − elseif conditions substituted by switch − case structures.

5   Case Study

In the preceding Section we discussed the limits of the existing data sets for clone detection and described how an artificial data set can be produced. Although such data set aims at training, we used it also to assess the Tree Kernel technique described in [9]. Even if we can not assume that the performance obtained on artificial data will generalize to the real case, these experiments allow us to obtain a better understanding of the force and weakness of a Kernel based clone detection approach.

Algorithm 2. Clone Generation Algorithm

Require: `function` : Target function/method of the analyzed system to clone;
Require: `type` : Type of the clone to generate;
Ensure: The artificially generated clone of the input function.
```
 1: function Clone(function, type)
            # This mutation operation holds for every Type of clones
 2:     clone ← CopyAndChangeLayout(function)
 3:     if type ≥ 2 then
            # This mutation operation is also applicable to Type 3 and Type 4 clones
 4:         SubstituteIdsAndLiterals(clone)
 5:     end if
 6:     if type = 3 then
 7:         AddOrDeleteStatements(clone)
 8:     else if type = 4 then
 9:         ReorderStatements(clone)
10:         SubstituteEquivalentControlStructures(clone)
11:     end if
12:     return clone
13: end function
```

5.1   Dataset

The considered target system is an academic application implemented in Java and developed by a Master student in Computer Science at the University of Naples "Federico II". As first step, the system has been manually analyzed to remove the clones introduced during implementation. Afterwards, we applied to this cleaned code the clone detector system we developed accordingly to the description in [9]. This is to verify whether it detected either any false clone or actual clones which had escaped the manual search. We then applied the clone generator on this system, limiting the generation of clones to Type 3, to make results comparable with ones reported in [9].

5.2   Research Questions and Variables

We assessed in this investigations the three following research questions:

RQ1 : Are the clones identified by the approach correct?
RQ2 : Is the group of clones identified by the approach complete?
RQ3 : Does the group of clones identified by the approach comply a good compromise between correctness and completeness?

Note that the definition of the third research question is motivated by the fact that the completeness requirement is opposite to the correctness one, as the former suggests outputting a large number of candidate clones, while the latter implies a more conservative approach, where only quite likely clones are detected.

Precision has been used to measure the correctness of the results, while the completeness has been assessed by employing the recall measure. More precisely, Precision (P) and Recall (R) are given by: ones:

$$P = \frac{\#\text{actual identified clones}}{\#\text{total candidates clones}}; \quad R = \frac{\#\text{actual identified clones}}{\#\text{total actual clones}}.$$

To assess whether the approach is effective (RQ3), we computed a version of the F-measure where Precision and Recall have the same weight, namely $F_1 = 2 * \frac{P*R}{P+R}$.

6   Results and Threats to Validity

In this section we discuss the results we gathered by the application of the approach on the different clone types, using different similarity thresholds for the detection. First the three research questions are addressed, then a discussion on how we handled the main threats to validity is presented.

Table 3. Summary statistics of the results

Clone Type	Threshold	Precision	Recall	F_1
Type 1	N.A.	1.0	1.0	1.0
Type 2	0.7	0.6	0.9	0.7
Type 2	0.8	0.7	0.6	0.6
Type 3	0.7	0.6	0.8	0.7
Type 3	0.8	0.6	0.8	0.7

6.1   Correctness, Completeness and Effectiveness of the Results

Since the Tree Kernel based approach does not include any formatting detail in its internal source code representation, Type 1 clones include no variability, and thus no Similarity threshold is necessary. With this kind of clones, it is easy to obtain 1.0 as F-Measure.

Regarding the other two types of clones, some modifications in the identifiers (Type 2 and 3) and in statements (Type 3 only) have been performed. In these cases, larger values of the threshold (e.g. 0.9) produce a small number of candidates. As a consequence, the recall is low, since only code fragments which are very similar are considered as clones. This effect is particularly evident for Type 3 clones, where no clones at all are detected. On the other hand, threshold values like 0.7 and 0.8 lead to better performance. In particular, the value 0.7 seems to improve completeness without affecting correctness, and is therefore preferable. Such attained results are strongly comparable with those reported in [9] in terms of all the three indicators we are considering, namely correctness, completeness and effectiveness, thus confirming the validity of artificially generated data.

6.2   Threats to Validity

We focused our attention in this section on the *construct validity* and the *external validity*. Construct validity threats concern the relationship between theory and observation. Precision, Recall, and F_1 well reflect the performance of the proposed approach. However, the used data set has been obtained by manually removing source clones and then introducing new clones of Types 1, 2 and 3 in a controlled way. The performed mutations may bias the results since they could affect the values of these measures. However, the defined mutation approach has been conceived to reduce this effect on the results as much as possible.

To increase our awareness on the achieved results we also plan to assess the validity of the results using different measures to determine various aspects of detection quality [4].

External validity threats regard the generalization of the results. An important threat is related to the studied software system. In particular, the size and the fact that the system was developed by a student may threaten the validity of the results. Also, the fact that this system was implemented in Java may affect the generalization of the results. To this aim, we plan to conduct case study replications on commercial software systems implemented in different programming language. This will increase our awareness on the validity of applying Kernels methods in the detection of software clones. Regarding the scalability, software systems with different size and clone density will be studied in the future.

7   Future Work: Architecture Recovery

Recovering the architecture of a software system requires to group together portions of code jointly performing a certain function and identifying the structural organization of these functional modules. The problem can be naturally formalized in terms of hierarchical clustering (see Section 2). Within such framework, we aim at improving over existing approaches by leveraging over the following aspects:

1) exploiting the rich structure characterizing software projects, in terms of hierarchical structuring of the code and relationships given by e.g. function calls. As already discussed for the clone detection problem (see Section 4), Kernel Methods are a natural candidate for learning problems involving richly structured objects. The promising results in clone detection using kernels on AST and PDG are encouraging, showing the potential of structured kernels in uncovering similarities between fragments. The wider variability of code found within functional modules requires an adaptation of kernels in order to effectively detect them. The problem can be addressed by combining kernel redesign with kernel learning approaches [19], where the similarity measure is not fully specified a-priori, but is learned from examples as a combination of similarity patterns (e.g. involving different types of lexical and structural information). Logic kernels [30,16] are particularly promising in this context, as they allow to encode arbitrary domain knowledge concerning relationships between code fragments from which similarity measures are to be learned.

2) exploiting all available information, in terms of existing full or partial architecture documentation, in order to improve performance of predictive algorithms. The few existing fully documented software systems can be used as gold standards representing how a correct architecture recovery should appear. The problem can be framed in terms of supervised clustering [15]: gold standards are examples of inputs (the code) and desired outputs (its architectural organization), used to train a predictive machine trying to approximate the desired output when fed with the code. In doing so, the predictor adapts the similarity measure to improve the approximation. When presented with a new piece of code, the trained machine clusters it using the learned similarity measure. We plan to extend this supervised clustering paradigm, mostly developed for flat clustering, to produce a hierarchy of clusters. Partial architecture documentation can also be used in a similar fashion by turning the supervised learning problem into a semi-supervised one: the algorithm is trained to output a full architectural representation which is consistent with the partial information available, possibly accounting for inconsistencies due to labeling errors or ambiguity.

8   Conclusions

Software Maintenance is a key phase of the Software development lifecycle, and consequently many research efforts are devoted to provide new solutions to improve its effectiveness. In this paper we dealt with the problem of developing automated approaches for addressing two typical Software Maintenance tasks, namely Software Architecture Recovery and Clone Detection. In particular we focused on Kernel methods, using them as a powerful and flexible tool for measuring "similarity" between code fragments, a main ingredient in clustering algorithms which are widely used in SAR and clone detection approaches. In particular, we presented promising results in clone detection using Tree Kernels over modified ASTs, together with a new method for the generation of labeled training sets. As for SAR, we discussed how to adapt our structured kernels to the problem at the hand, suggesting a number of directions to leverage the full power of structured-output machine learning techniques.

References

1. Anquetil, N., Fourrier, C., Lethbridge, T.C.: Experiments with clustering as a software remodularization method. In: Proceedings of the 6th Working Conference on Reverse Engineering, pp. 235–255. IEEE Computer Society, Washington, DC (1999)
2. Baker, B.: On finding duplication and near-duplication in large software systems. In: IEEE Proceedings of the Working Conference on Reverse Engineering (1995)
3. Baxter, I.D., Yahin, A., Moura, L., Sant'Anna, M., Bier, L.: Clone detection using abstract syntax trees. In: Proceedings of the International Conference on Software Maintenance, pp. 368–377. IEEE Press (1998)

4. Bellon, S., Koschke, R., Antoniol, G., Krinke, J., Merlo, E.M.: Comparison and evaluation of clone detection tools. IEEE Trans. Software Eng., 577–591 (September 2007)
5. Bittencourt, R.A., Guerrero, D.D.S.: Comparison of graph clustering algorithms for recovering software architecture module views. In: Proceedings of the European Conference on Software Maintenance and Reengineering, pp. 251–254. IEEE Computer Society, Washington, DC (2009),
   http://portal.acm.org/citation.cfm?id=1545011.1545446
6. Bulychev, P., Minea, M.: Duplicate code detection using anti-unification. In: Spring/Summer Young Researcher's Colloquium (2008)
7. Corazza, A., Di Martino, S., Maggio, V., Scanniello, G.: Investigating the use of lexical information for software system clustering. In: Proceedings of the 15th European Conference on Software Maintenance and Reengineering, CSMR 2011, pp. 35–44. IEEE Computer Society, Washington, DC (2011),
   http://dx.doi.org/10.1109/CSMR.2011.8
8. Corazza, A., Di Martino, S., Scanniello, G.: A probabilistic based approach towards software system clustering. In: Proceedings of the European Conference on Software Maintenance and Reengineering, pp. 88–96 (2010)
9. Corazza, A., Di Martino, S., Maggio, V., Scanniello, G.: A tree kernel based approach for clone detection. In: Proceedings of the 2010 IEEE International Conference on Software Maintenance, ICSM 2010, pp. 1–5. IEEE Computer Society, Washington, DC (2010),
   http://dx.doi.org/10.1109/ICSM.2010.5609715
10. Corazza, A., Di Martino, S., Maggio, V., Scanniello, G.: Combining machine learning and information retrieval techniques for software clustering. In: Moschitti, A., Scandariato, R. (eds.) EternalS 2011. CCIS, vol. 255, pp. 42–60. Springer, Heidelberg (2012)
11. Deerwester, S.C., Dumais, S.T., Landauer, T.K., Furnas, G.W., Harshman, R.A.: Indexing by latent semantic analysis. Journal of the American Society of Information Science 41(6), 391–407 (1990),
    http://citeseerx.ist.psu.edu/viewdoc/summary?doi=10.1.1.49.7546
12. Doval, D., Mancoridis, S., Mitchell, B.S.: Automatic clustering of software systems using a genetic algorithm. In: Proceedings of the Software Technology and Engineering Practice, pp. 73–82. IEEE Computer Society, Washington, DC (1999),
    http://portal.acm.org/citation.cfm?id=829540.832036
13. Ducasse, S., Pollet, D.: Software architecture reconstruction: A process-oriented taxonomy. IEEE Transactions on Software Engineering 35(4), 573–591 (2009)
14. Ducasse, S., Rieger, M., Demeyer, S.: A language independent approach for detecting duplicated code. In: Proceedings of the International Conference on Software Maintenance, pp. 109–118 (1999)
15. Finley, T., Joachims, T.: Supervised clustering with support vector machines. In: Proceedings of the 22nd International Conference on Machine Learning, ICML 2005, pp. 217–224. ACM, New York (2005),
    http://doi.acm.org/10.1145/1102351.1102379
16. Frasconi, P., Passerini, A.: Learning with kernels and logical representations. In: De Raedt, L., Frasconi, P., Kersting, K., Muggleton, S. (eds.) Probabilistic Inductive Logic Programming. LNCS (LNAI), vol. 4911, pp. 56–91. Springer, Heidelberg (2008)

17. Gabel, M., Jiang, L., Su, Z.: Scalable detection of semantic clones. In: Proceedings of the 30th International Conference on Software Engineering, ICSE 2008, pp. 321–330. ACM, New York (2008), http://doi.acm.org/10.1145/1368088.1368132

18. Garlan, D.: Software architecture: a roadmap. In: Proceedings of the Conference on the Future of Software Engineering, ICSE 2000, pp. 91–101. ACM, New York (2000), http://doi.acm.org/10.1145/336512.336537

19. Gönen, M., Alpaydin, E.: Multiple kernel learning algorithms. J. Mach. Learn. Res., 2211–2268 (July 2011)

20. Hofmann, T., Schölkopf, B., Smola, A.J.: Kernel methods in machine learning. Annals of Statistics 36(3), 1171–1220 (2008), http://www.projecteuclid.org/DPubS?verb=Displayversion= 1.0service=UIhandle=euclid.aos/1211819561page=record

21. Jiang, L., Misherghi, G., Su, Z., Glondu, S.: Deckard: Scalable and accurate tree-based detection of code clones. In: Proceedings of the 29th International Conference on Software Engineering, ICSE 2007, pp. 96–105. IEEE Computer Society, Washington, DC (2007), http://dx.doi.org/10.1109/ICSE.2007.30

22. Johnson, J.H.: Identifying redundancy in source code using fingerprints. In: Proc. Conf. Centre for Advanced Studies on Collaborative Research (CASCON), pp. 171–183. IBM Press (1993)

23. Kamiya, T., Kusumoto, S., Inoue, K.: Ccfinder: A multilinguistic token-based code clone detection system for large scale source code. IEEE Trans. Software Eng. 28(7), 654–670 (2002)

24. Kleinberg, J.M.: Authoritative sources in a hyperlinked environment. Journal of the ACM 46, 604–632 (1999), http://doi.acm.org/10.1145/324133.324140

25. Komondoor, R., Horwitz, S.: Using slicing to identify duplication in source code. In: Cousot, P. (ed.) SAS 2001. LNCS, vol. 2126, pp. 40–56. Springer, Heidelberg (2001)

26. Koschke, R.: Atomic architectural component recovery for program understanding and evolution. Softwaretechnik-Trends (2000), http://www.iste.uni-stuttgart.de/ps/rainer/thesis

27. Koschke, R., Falke, R., Frenzel, P.: Clone detection using abstract syntax suffix trees. In: WCRE 2006: Proceedings of the 13th Working Conference on Reverse Engineering, pp. 253–262. IEEE Computer Society, Washington, DC (2006)

28. Krinke, J.: Identifying Similar Code with Program Dependence Graphs. In: Proc. Working Conf. Reverse Engineering (WCRE), pp. 301–309. IEEE Computer Society Press (2001)

29. Kuhn, A., Ducasse, S., Gírba, T.: Semantic clustering: Identifying topics in source code. Information and Software Technology 49, 230–243 (2007), http://portal.acm.org/citation.cfm?id=1224560.1224698

30. Landwehr, N., Passerini, A., Raedt, L., Frasconi, P.: Fast learning of relational kernels. Mach. Learn. 78(3), 305–342 (2010), http://dx.doi.org/10.1007/s10994-009-5163-1

31. Lehman, M.M.: Programs, life cycles, and laws of software evolution. Proc. IEEE 68(9), 1060–1076 (1980)

32. Leitão, A.M.: Detection of redundant code using r^2d^2. Software Quality Journal 12(4), 361–382 (2004)

33. Maletic, J.I., Marcus, A.: Supporting program comprehension using semantic and structural information. In: Proceedings of the 23rd International Conference on Software Engineering, ICSE 2001, pp. 103–112. IEEE Computer Society, Washington, DC (2001), http://portal.acm.org/citation.cfm?id=381473.381484

34. Maqbool, O., Babri, H.: Hierarchical clustering for software architecture recovery. IEEE Transactions on Software Engineering 33(11), 759–780 (2007)
35. Menchetti, S., Costa, F., Frasconi, P.: Weighted decomposition kernels. In: Proceedings of the 22nd International Conference on Machine Learning, ICML 2005, pp. 585–592. ACM, New York (2005), http://doi.acm.org/10.1145/1102351.1102425
36. Mitchell, B.S., Mancoridis, S.: On the automatic modularization of software systems using the bunch tool. IEEE Transactions on Software Engineering 32, 193–208 (2006), http://portal.acm.org/citation.cfm?id=1128600.1128815
37. Moschitti, A., Basili, R., Pighin, D.: Tree Kernels for Semantic Role Labeling. In: Computational Linguistics, pp. 193–224. MIT Press, Cambridge (2008)
38. Risi, M., Scanniello, G., Tortora, G.: Using fold-in and fold-out in the architecture recovery of software systems. Formal Asp. Comput. 24(3), 307–330 (2012)
39. Roy, C.K., Cordy, J.R.: Nicad: Accurate detection of near-miss intentional clones using flexible pretty-printing and code normalization. In: ICPC, pp. 172–181 (2008)
40. Roy, C.K., Cordy, J.R., Koschke, R.: Comparison and evaluation of code clone detection techniques and tools: A qualitative approach. Sci. Comput. Program. 74(7), 470–495 (2009)
41. Scanniello, G., D'Amico, A., D'Amico, C., D'Amico, T.: Architectural layer recovery for software system understanding and evolution. Software Practice and Experience 40, 897–916 (2010), http://dx.doi.org/10.1002/spe.v40:10
42. Scanniello, G., D'Amico, A., D'Amico, C., D'Amico, T.: Using the kleinberg algorithm and vector space model for software system clustering. In: Proceedings of the IEEE 18th International Conference on Program Comprehension, ICPC 2010, pp. 180–189. IEEE Computer Society, Washington, DC (2010), http://dx.doi.org/10.1109/ICPC.2010.17
43. Tzerpos, V., Holt, R.C.: On the stability of software clustering algorithms. In: Proceedings of the 8th International Workshop on Program Comprehension, pp. 211–218 (2000)
44. Vert, J.P.: A Tree Kernel to analyse phylogenetic profiles. Bioinformatics 18(suppl. 1), S276–S284 (2002)
45. Wahler, V., Seipel, D., von Gudenberg, J.W., Fischer, G.: Clone detection in source code by frequent itemset techniques. In: SCAM 2004: Proceedings of the Fourth IEEE International Workshop on Source Code Analysis and Manipulation, pp. 128–135. IEEE Computer Society, Washington, DC (2004)
46. Wiggerts, T.A.: Using clustering algorithms in legacy systems remodularization. In: Proceedings of the Fourth Working Conference on Reverse Engineering (WCRE 1997), pp. 33–43. IEEE Computer Society, Washington, DC (1997), http://portal.acm.org/citation.cfm?id=832304.836999
47. Wu, J., Hassan, A.E., Holt, R.C.: Comparison of clustering algotithms in the context of software evolution. In: Proceedings of the 21st IEEE International Conference on Software Maintenance, pp. 525–535. IEEE Computer Society (2005)
48. Yang, W.: Identifying syntactic differences between two programs. Software - Practice and Experience 21(7), 739–755 (1991)

The EternalS Roadmap – Defining a Research Agenda for Eternal Systems

Robert Mullins

Waterford Institute of Technology

Abstract. Science, technology and business are increasingly dependent on software. This trend is driven by increasing system size, complexity, diversity and flexibility and the obligation for tailored integration of end-users, processes and evolving technologies. The complexity scale of current systems exceeds our current understanding of systems engineering and the number of system parameters to be controlled as part of the overall design process exceeds the performance of the associated tools and techniques we are using. This leads to excessive costs for software maintenance and system degradation over its lifetime. The tools and techniques must evolve to take into account this increasing systems, software and architecture scale and complexity. Software intensive systems must be flexible to accommodate a range of requirements and operating conditions, and capable of evolving to allow these parameters to change over time. Software Engineering approaches to reusability and maintenance must cope with the dynamics and longevity of future software applications and infrastructures, e.g., for the Future Internet, e-commerce, e-health, and egovernment. The EternalS project is developing a roadmap for the next two decades to inspire a research agenda for software and systems engineering to help address these issues. This paper presents some of the key issues outlined above, the roadmapping process and some of the key findings to date.

Keywords: Roadmap, Software Engineering, Eternal Systems.

1 Introduction

This paper presents the Eternal Systems research communitys analysis on the key technologies, methodologies and processes supporting the development and maintenance of large, complex, mission critical and long lived software systems, and its perspective on the priorities for the future systems engineering research under the European Commissions (ECs) Framework Program 8 (FP8). The scope covers the vision, challenges and research needs for each of the eternal systems areas as identified by the EternalS project, a Coordination Action supported by the 7th Framework Programme of the EC within the FET (Future and Emerging Technologies) scheme.

Changing user requirements, operating conditions and technologies continue to be an issue for all stages of the systems development including its maintenance.

A. Moschitti and B. Plank (Eds.): EternalS 2013, CCIS 379, pp. 135–147, 2013.

This is the context into which future research must deliver and take into account that systems need to adapt to changes in user requirements and application domains.

Much research in software engineering have been focused on improving software quality and automating the maintenance process to reduce software costs and mitigate complications associated with the evolution process. Despite all the effort expended in this area, these are still high cost and effort activities, software still continues to be unreliable, and software bugs can wreak havoc on software producers and consumers alike. The EternalS group has identified a number of key disciplines that they believe can make a very positive contribution to advancing research against this background. These include Variability Management through Software Product Line Engineering, Software Lifecycle, Adaptation and Time awareness through Model Centric and Driven Design, and Machine Learning as an enabler for the evolution and selfadaptability of software.

2   Technology Roadmap

The possibilities of technology are often analysed in an isolated manner by those with expert knowledge exclusively in that field. These forecasters tend to trace straight lines into the future, that project the present, assuming that the current context is perennial and fundamentals are invariant and durable. They generally forget about inevitable disruptions such as major scientific breakthroughs or game changing technology. These would appear to be likely and expected, if the forecasters considered the larger picture, not only of their specific area of study, but also taking into account the entire landscape.

Any engineered products, including software, should be viewed from a business perspective, not just from a technological one. Of particular interest are:

- Proven and emerging business models: software as a product, software as a service, mobile applications ecosystems, open source;
- The intersection of software engineering with the software business: business perspectives on technologies such as cloud computing, requirements engineering and software architecture;
- Outsourcing: long-term economic implications, new models;
- The software business in public administrations: strategies and approaches for maximizing the public value of software;
- Public support for the software business: initiatives at the government level to stimulate or shape the software business, including standards and specifications;
- The software-intensive product: the evolving business context as software increasingly replaces hardware in products, ranging from regulatory implications in safety- critical environments (e.g., health, automotive) to the impact on market positioning as new powerfully featured, software-driven products blur the distinction between traditional segments.

The roadmapping process attempts to map out a path over a period of time, taking into account the perspectives outlined above and also taking account of at least expected developments which could have a material impact during the period under consideration. This is what the EternalS project is undertaking and the results of the project will be documented via the roadmaps. The plan has been for three versions of the roadmaps deliverables for the project to be produced. Two have already been produced; the first version, D2.1 was created in July 2011 and the second D2.2 was created in April 2012. A number of EU funded FET (Future and Emerging Technology) projects (CONNECT, HATS, Living-Knowledge, and Secure Change) which are oriented towards research which is of relevance to Eternal systems, have been involved in the EternalS roadmapping process and have contributed to the roadmap deliverables. The TSSG research group, part of Waterford Institute of Technology leads the roadmap activity as editors and contributors.

3 A Vision for Eternal Systems Research

A software system must evolve, or it becomes progressively less satisfactory. The question of how to cope with imposed or induced change is particularly challenging in the context of trends driving the Future Internet. At the infrastructure level, the Future Internet will leverage new technologies and protocols to promote the convergence of traditional and small/portable devices on a much larger scale than present. At the service level, systems will no longer be able to address a closed universe of stakeholders. Additionally, market forces, technological innovation and new business models will push system fragmentation even further.

On the other hand, those complex, fragmented systems of the Future Internet (or at least parts of them) are expected to be operational for a very long time. Design and implementation decisions must be made in a broad context, considering long-term goals under the constraint of currently available resources and technologies. To cope with these challenges, long-living Future Internet Systems need to be exceptionally flexible. They will have to constantly evolve to adjust to the changing requirements. However, evolution represents a constant threat to the systems quality. Since largescale, long lived software-based systems (Eternal Systems) increasingly pervade our daily life and put an ever rising number of digital assets at risk, it is a topic of greater significance. The questions of how to build and manage Eternal Systems leads to a broad array of research challenges. In recent years, there have been a lot of studies aimed at characterizing the evolution of a software system. Many of these studies analyse the behaviour of a variable over a given period of observation. How does the size of a software system evolve? What about its complexity? Does the number of defects increase over time or does it remain stable?

These lead to a number of key focus areas in software intensive and systems engineering:

- Models - the need to enumerate and classify modelling dimensions for obtaining precise models to support run-time reasoning and decision making for achieving evolvable need compliance;
- Requirements - the need to define a new requirements language for handling uncertainty to give flexible and self-adaptive systems the freedom to do adaptation;
- Variability - over the last number of years there has been an explosion in the number of devices that use software, ranging from the obvious (mobile phones, consumer electronics) to the less obvious (medical implants, vehicles). The processes and methodologies required to create, test and deploy software for such vast numbers and purposes, and manage reusability need to be developed.
- Engineering - the need to consider feedback control loops as first-class entities during engineering of flexible and self-adaptive systems;
- Security - this must be an integral part of all software and systems in an increasingly open and connected ecosystem.
- Assurances - the need to define novel verification and validation methods for the provision of assurances that cover the flexibility and self-adaptation of systems.
- Evolution and Self adaptability - Systems that can automatically detect and adapt themselves to their environment and changes to their environment. The belief is that machine learning is the key to this capability.

Recent software evolution studies rely on fine-grained information mined by integrating several kinds of repositories, such as versioning systems, bug tracking systems, or mailing lists. Nowadays, many other sources of information, ranging from code search repositories, vulnerability databases, informal communications, and legal documents are also being considered. This would possibly aid to capture the rationale of some events occurring in a software project, and link them to statistical relations observed.

The road towards shifting from solid empirical models towards principles of software evolution will likely be long and difficult, therefore we should prepare ourselves to traverse it and go as far as possible. To do this, we need to pay attention to:

1. Combining quantitative studies with qualitative studies, surveys, and informal interviews,
2. Using appropriate statistical and machine learning techniques able to capture the temporal relation among different events, introducing robustness and adaptability and
3. Making extensive use of natural language processing and text mining to automatically process the various sources of information available

4   Key Research Topics

The following sections document the key research technologies, processes and methodologies identified by the EternalS project as being relevant to the future research of Eternal Systems. These are looked at under the headings the software engineering challenges of managing diversity among multiple systems that are essentially similar but slightly different, managing the evolution over time of long lived systems and finally examining machine learning as a means of addressing some of the key issues found in the aforementioned areas.

4.1   Managing Diversity

Diversity impacts all phases of software development and leads to an increase in complexity, because variability has to be anticipated in requirements analysis, design, implementation, and validation stages.

The key methodology supporting software diversity management is Software Product Line Engineering (SPLE). Software intensive systems in certain domains may share a large amount of commonalities. Instead of developing each product individually, SPLE looks at these systems as a whole and develops them by maximizing the scale of reuse of platforms and mass customization. It is claimed that SPLE can help reduce both development cost and time to market. A key distinction of SPLE from other reuse-based approaches is that the various assets of the product line infrastructure contain variability, which refers to the ability of an artefact to be configured, customized, extended, or changed for use in a specific context.

Variability in a product line must be defined, represented, exploited, implemented, and evolved throughout the lifecycle of SPLE, which is called Variability Management (VM). This has been studied for almost 20 years since the early 1990s. Feature- Oriented Domain Analysis (FODA) method and the Synthesis approach were two of the first contributions to VM research and practice.

SPLE is a two-stage process which is split into a family engineering and an application engineering phase. During family engineering, the scope of the product line is defined by determining which products should be included in the product line. Reusable artefacts are then developed and stored in the product line artefact database. During application engineering, the product line artefacts are customized and assembled in order to realize a given product configuration.

4.2   Managing the Software Lifecycle

The question on how to build and manage long-lived security-critical systems, leads to a broad array of challenges, two of which are mentioned below. The first one refers to the engineering process: how should stakeholders (e.g., end users, business analysts, requirements analysts, system architects etc.) cope with the various aspects of change that may come with the evolution of long-living systems? Current process models have considerable shortcomings: security is only integrated superficially, runtime adaptability is not addressed at all, model and runtime artifacts are hardly kept consistent.

The second challenge refers to the architecture and implementation of Future Internet Systems: how could such systems be designed and realized so that they are flexible enough to evolve over time accommodating the various changes? Promising approaches can be found in the area of pattern-based and model-driven engineering with a broad set of formal, semi-formal and informal techniques for the transformation of models, the deployment and (re)configuration of components, functional and nonfunctional testing, and the verification of properties.

Software architectures are the main blueprints of software systems and need to be designed from the ground up to accommodate evolution. To date this has not been the case and even if an architecture is put in place, changes and modifications during both the development process and post deployment evolution may introduce architectural decay. These changes are seldom updated in documentation.

To deal with this almost universal software engineering challenge, over the last 10-15 years a number of model-centric, model-driven (collectively called MD*) approaches have been proposed. The vision of this approach is that systems are described at the level of abstract models, often with the help of graphical notation. Code is not written by hand, but automatically generated and evolved from the models. The converse of this is also possible and models can be automatically learned from the codebase and a representative set of execution traces. This is known as Software Architecture Recovery (SAR) and is described below. This makes it possible to deal with legacy systems and to (self-) adapt to new environments more easily. Because code generation does not come with any correctness guarantees, an important aspect of research of the model centric approach is formal verification.

Complementary to MD, it is also possible to automatically reconstruct models from the codebase and, possibly, a representative set of execution traces. SAR is the process of focusing on recovering the high-level design of a system from its source code. SAR processes and tools use both static and dynamic analysis. Concerning static analysis, clustering techniques and other heuristics (e.g., based on naming conventions) are often applied to the source code and configuration files to create a representation for the architecture and to identify software patterns. The quality and accuracy of the results is typically improved when dynamic analysis is also used, e.g., by looking at representative execution traces, as well as system logs. This is particularly important with Object Oriented programs, which employ polymorphism in ways which may not be obvious from the source. Other areas such as resource usage can also be relevant to understanding the architecture.

4.3   Middleware and Cloud Computing

Distributed systems are experiencing a period of rapid and intense change, at a rate that is unprecedented since the inception of the area in the early 1980s.

With the advent of cloud computing, we can see the deployment of very large-scale distributed systems offering a range of novel and exciting new services, including interesting new paradigms for large-scale computation. Furthermore, distributed systems are becoming significantly more heterogeneous spanning very small devices embedded in the physical environment around us through data centres housing massive cluster computers. Users of distributed systems are often mobile, resulting in significant context changes over time, which the system must adapt to. Networking technologies continue to evolve with, for example, the emergence of a range of new ad hoc networking techniques and peer-to-peer approaches to implementing core network services.

Distributed systems are also being challenged by the new styles of applications and services now being considered. A key illustration of this is the rapid emergence of social computing, that is supporting social behaviours in distributed systems through tools such as wikis, blogs and social networking sites. Social computing is also now being taken a step further as the associated tools exploit the emergence of mobile devices and also start to embrace the new potential offered by ubiquitous computing.

Security is a key concern in Cloud Computing. The common use of virtualization introduces a new layer between software and hardware and this in turn introduces a new layer which can be potentially compromised. Other concerns with cloud include managing and verifying the identity of the clients who use cloud infrastructure, privacy of data contained in the cloud, physical access and security concerns for the remote hardware, availability of resources and legal issues as cloud technology separates the physical location from where the services are being used.

4.4   Security

Security is increasingly becoming a fundamental part of software development rather than simply a functional requirement. It is becoming understood that with increasingly open and networked systems, security is a primary system requirement and it needs to be designed into the software from the ground up, and needs to be examined and addressed on an on-going basis, as the environment evolves and new types of threats become apparent.

Risk Management is key to the process of assessing and managing the security risks associated with the software systems of an organisation and planning how to deal with events that may occur. This is a particularly important process for eternal systems as by their nature, both the systems and their environment evolve over their (long) lifetimes, and the risks faced change and the risk management process needs to handle this change and also adapt as new risks occur and older risks are no longer relevant. For this reason, to be effective, risk analysis is an on-going requirement.

A new branch of software engineering, Security Software Engineering focuses on integrating security-centric processes (including awareness and training) into all aspects of the software development process. In particular, the focus of the research community is shifting towards dealing with security concerns as early as possible in the development process, i.e., starting from the requirements and risk analysis, as well as the architectural and detailed design. An explicit representation of security needs and security mechanisms is the stepping stone to systematically support the evolution of security in Eternal Systems.

4.5   Adaptation and Awareness through Machine Learning

The simultaneous explosion of information, the integration of technology, and the continuous evolution from software-intensive systems to ultra-large-scale systems require new and innovative approaches for building, running, and managing software systems. Self-adaptation - systems that are able to adjust their behaviour in response to their perception of the environment and the system itself has become an important research topic.

Adaptation can be seen as an intelligent function that can automatically select different functionalities, e.g., by composing different software components. Such function can hardly be based on predefined handcrafted rules since predicting the future working conditions caused by changes in the environment or in the user requirements is too complex. As previously mentioned ML owns two important properties; it can:

- learn its function models using millions of variables, accurately describing the system and environment conditions; and
- use a probabilistic characterization of the environment to produce the most effective evolution choice. Such management of uncertainty also produces evolution functions that are robust to unexpected conditions.

However, the use of ML requires the modelling of system and environment conditions in terms of input objects for the target learning algorithm. As previously mentioned structural kernels can help the definition of such objects. The most comprehensive examples of the use of kernels can be found in automatic extraction tools that harvest the unstructured data sources that abound on the web.

5   Future Research

5.1   Diversity Awareness

In the early phases of software development, such as requirements, the anticipated diversity of the set of systems to be developed has to be discovered and specified by suitable modelling approaches. Current practice captures variability at the requirements level mainly by domain models, feature models or by decision-oriented modelling concepts. This so called problem space variability is well understood and can be rigorously analysed by mathematical means. However, it is mostly disconnected from solution space variability that has to be formulated in terms of the reusable development artefacts. This highlights the need for new variability modelling techniques that can be integrated into a model-based development process for diverse systems. In this model-based development process, the variability of the set of systems to be developed should be traceable from the product features via different abstraction layers to the actual implementation level.

The importance of validation and verification cannot be under estimated. Methods to guarantee essential system qualities, such as integrity, consistency, correctness, and efficiency, are essential for diverse systems. Diversity increases system complexity which leads to a greater risk for system failures. Moreover, the complexity introduced by diversity makes quality assurance even more complicated as for single systems. Hence, incremental and compositional verification and validation techniques have to be devised to deal with the special requirements of diversity.

Ensuring software integrity is of prime importance. Given the critical nature of eternal systems, it is very important that software can validate itself and ensure that has not been changed or compromised by an external party. This can be quite a challenge particularly in the case of SPLE where so many legitimate variants of a software system can exist and where software may also be built with the capability to self-adapt. This challenge will be addressed through research in the area of automated test case generation and formal testing in SPLE in product derivation and application engineering.

5.2   The Software Lifecycle and Evolution

There is a strong requirement in software engineering to improve the evolution management process to ensure that software artefacts are kept consistent over systems evolution. It is envisioned that machine learning can influence software evolution and will lead to new testing approaches that are more pragmatic. This requires interdisciplinary research for instance information retrieval (for documents, images, etc.). These advances will improve the evolution management process by ensuring that the artefacts (requirements, architecture, etc.) are kept consistent over time.

There is a need to advance the state of the art of Software Engineering in the areas of managing the evolution of software architectures and their corresponding implementations. To this end, the abstract modelling of software architectures and corresponding code generation promises a real breakthrough in the way we produce and think about software systems. However, the state of the art is characterized by a number of challenges that yet have to be overcome as investigated in Model-Driven Engineering, and spanning support for Model-to-Model, Model-to-Code and Models@ Runtime. Some of these are:

- There are many modelling formalisms, but as yet no "end-to-end" approach that takes evolvability into account.
- Code generation is often from CASE tools is partial and needs to be completed in a manual process. Full automation of code generation and formal verification methods to prove correctness need to be developed.
- There is as yet no systematic link between development processes and modelling languages.

– Development methods should be applicable to the growing number of safetycritical applications (e.g., in the embedded systems area), which in many cases require certification.

Future research directions include combining abstract modelling, diversity, time awareness and machine learning to address problems of future software systems. It has been established that there are several overlaps and common interests between the areas of software evolution and adaptation, diversity management and machine learning which are fruitful for future research. Machine learning techniques can be employed to improve the diversity and evolution management of software to handle their configuration, collaboration, and adaptation issues.

5.3   Cloud Computing and Middleware

Manageability in the cloud environment is a major challenge, where manageability is defined as "the collective processes of deployment, configuration, optimization, and administration during the lifecycle of IT systems and services". Intrinsic to this are the security issues associated with cloud computing. This becomes particularly important when some of the main applications enabled through the cloud; enterprise computing, Web 2.0 and High Performance Computing are considered.

While many observers of cloud computing tend to emphasise the computing on demand and data storage elements of cloud infrastructure, there is also an important role for distributed computing in the cloud. While cloud computing often assumes a certain level of homogeneity in applications and execution environments, in reality there can be high levels of heterogeneity in the nature of the underlying clusters and also in the workloads imposed by the applications. This places heavy demands on the underlying scheduling algorithms underpinning cloud computation services. The emergence of technologies such as MapReduce highlights the key research challenges associated with heterogeneity particularly for job scheduling. There are also implications of heterogeneity for other cloud services.

Middleware in this type of massively distributed infrastructure also raises some new research topics. What are the right abstractions for the development of future distributed systems given the scale of complexity of the underlying infrastructure? How can we abstract over this complexity? What do we need in terms of middleware APIs, programming languages and associated software engineering methodologies? How do we achieve interoperability and openness in this new world we find ourselves in, especially given the extreme heterogeneity we encounter in the distributed systems of today? What principles and approaches do we need to deal with such extreme heterogeneity? Do existing approaches to interoperability and openness still work?

5.4   Security

Risk Management as described above is a key process in securing software systems. Currently, risk analysis is a manual and time consuming process and as such creating methodologies and finding ways of automating this process is a good candidate for research within the context of Eternal Systems. Some existing research work has been completed and some tools (CORAS, Proseco) are available in this area. The SecureChange project, part of the Forever Yours group of FET projects has completed some research in the area of systematic processes for risk analysis.

Security and how it is applied to the various branches of Cloud Computing will continue to be a very important area of research with immediate practical applications.

5.5   Machine Learning

The key challenge for Machine Learning in the context of Eternal Systems is to develop methods that allow systems to adapt and evolve as their environment changes. For instance, we may encounter problems such as:

- Adaptation of legacy systems.
- Reconciliation of systems whose interfaces are evolving.
- Introduction of new components in an existing environment before and after
- Automatic risk analysis to deal with evolving security concerns.

Machine-learned systems may need to evolve as the distribution of the data on which they operate evolves. This is particularly true for natural language processing systems since new terms frequently enter the vocabulary. Component-based systems need adaptation mechanisms as partly incompatible components are introduced and some components become obsolete.

A further research area is the automatic application of user requirements by means of natural language processing. The latter can automatically interpret the modifications in user requirements and convert them in actions to make evolve software system, e.g., by selecting new components in the system.

An important area where ML can be brought to bear on software engineering and variability management is automated test case generation and execution. This would help solve the major problem of testing in SPLE for product derivation and application engineering use cases

Further Machine Learning challenges in the domain of software engineering of Eternal Systems include:

- Researching the correct criteria for the selection of state of the art machine learning techniques such as Finite State Automata and Kernel Methods, particularly Support Vector Machines and their application to real world problem domains that today can only be addressed with simplified or inadequate models.

– Resolving differences in current approaches and seeking reconciliation between the approaches of automata learning and kernel methods to produce a universal model.
– Application of machine learning techniques to learn systems behaviour and semantics and thereby assist automated software composition

Difficulty Level					
Research Challenge	1	2	3	4	5
Variability Modeling			*		
Formal Verification Methods					*
Automated Test Case Generation		*			
Model Driven Design			*		
Advances in Code Generation Technologies				*	
Middleware for massively distributed computing			*		
Automated Risk Management				*	
Security Software Engineering	*				
Software Adaptation through ML				*	
Natural Language Requirements Definition					*
Reconciliation between Kernel methods and automata based AI			*		

Fig. 1. Table outlining broad research challenges and estimated difficulty to achieve tangible results, rated from 1 to 5

6   Conclusion

This paper gives an overview of the EternalS project and the roadmapping process, its objectives and a summary of the main areas of focus. Certain key areas of software engineering are introduced and their relevance to Eternal Systems is explained. Machine Learning is introduced as a potentially effective tool to help address some of the core challenges. The main future research areas are discussed at some length and topics which would be considered to be both valuable and interesting in their respective areas are outlined. For more information, the

EternalS roadmapping deliverable discusses and elaborates on the topics mentioned above in much greater detail.

Acknowledgements. This work has been co-financed by the European Commission - IST EternalS (FP7- 247758). Apart from this, the European Commission has no responsibility for the content of this paper. The information in this document is provided as is and no guarantee or warranty is given that the information is fit for any particular purpose. The user thereof uses the information at its sole risk and liability.

References

1. Voelter, M., Groher, I.: Product Line Implementation using Aspect-Oriented and Model-Driven Software Development (2006)
2. Kalawsky, R.S.: Grand Challenges for Systems Engineering Research. In: 7th Annual Conference on Systems Engineering Research 2009 (2009)
3. Tao, Q., Chu, D.-J., Wang, J.: Recursive Support Vector Machines for Dimensionality Reduction. IEEE Trans. Neural Networks 19(1), 189–193 (2008)
4. Simon, H.: Why Should Machines Learn? In: Michalski, R., Carbonell, J., Mitchell, T. (eds.) Machine Learning: An Artificial Intelligence Approach, pp. 25–38. Tioga Press (1983)
5. Lin, Y.: Support Vector Machines and the Bayes Rule in Classification. Data Mining and Knowledge Discovery 6(3), 259–275 (2002)

Author Index

Author Index